Praise fo

"Hum of the Home is useful in cultivating a spiritual, practical, and hospitable atmosphere within the home. Leah Simpson guides the reader through the basics of domestic skills, but focuses on the heart of the home – love. This is a **must read** for those looking for constructive ways to organize household affairs. Supremely practical, *Hum of the Home* offers a wealth of ideas for those who desire to honor God by taking care of their family and serving others with contagious hospitality."

Samuel W. "Dub" Oliver, Ph.D.
President of Union University, Jackson, TN

"There is a sweet and comforting power in the humming of one who is fulfilled and content. Leah Simpson is a compelling woman of God, a wonderful wife, a dedicated, loving, wise mother of eleven children. Five of these children she homeschooled and discipled into adulthood while the other six are in heaven. Read her many creative, fun and wise ideas to enrich your life as a wife, a mother, or educator, or as you keep your home. Read and learn as you listen to her beautiful *Hum of the Home!"*

"Lana Harris Thornton"
THEA (Tennessee Home Education Association) Event Coordinator
Ambassadors for Christ Speech & Debate Club, Administrator &
Tournament Director
HSLDA Compassion TN Ambassador

Hum of the Home

Hum of the Home
Rhythms and Routines of Homemaking

Ideas for a Clean and Orderly Home

Leah Vance Simpson

ISBN: 978-1-7336554-0-8

Dedicated to my husband Tim
who inspires me with courage to live my dreams

Tim & Leah.

…and to the children who I dearly love.
They are the reason for my hum.

Table of Contents

Introduction

Recently, I spent the day with a friend at the Hummingbird Festival nearby. The rapid action of these delicate creatures combined the purring sound and steady vibration reminded me of the hum we often experience in our homes. When our homes are humming, they are full of activity.

The buzzing around can be chaotic or like a purr which is steady and rhythmic. I often pause to listen to the humming in my home. Do you? Is it a sound that brings you joy? Do the routines and rhythms of your everyday patterns create order?

Hummingbird.

Homemaking is a journey of our hearts. God calls us to be our best selves at home, not only out in public. Home is one of God's best ideas. He created his most intricate creations to live together as families. Why? We know that God wants our best, so he places us in this cocoon of nurturing and growing. He uses the family structure to demonstrate His love to us as his children.

The alliance of a strong family with unbreakable bonds is one of our most valuable gifts. Making a home requires both physical and emotional work. It is intentional. To be called to the construction of such labor should merit honor. If you are reading this book, you are likely responsible in some fashion for a home and your people.

Mom & Daphne & me.

This is a collection of what I learned from being raised by a brilliant, Godly mother. Wisdom grew from conversations with God as I poured over my Bible and lived beside the clever women I met along my homemaking, wife-ing and mothering journey. I am truly grateful. My mother actually graduated with a degree in Home Economics and Secondary Education. Naturally, she implemented the practical work of home making along with the spiritual activity of growing her children almost seamlessly. This book mentions my mother frequently because she is the "why" behind much of this book. However, my belief is that God created a natural bent toward these nurturing patterns in those called to do the work of homemaking.

In my childhood, my parents served as church planters in St. Lucia, West Indies; Hilo, Hawaii and later in Pukalani, Maui and Abbotsford, British Columbia. They also served in short-term mission station supply in Scotland, Finland, Ireland, Alaska and Ontario, Canada. In fifty-two years of ministry my parents shepherded and pastored twelve churches. During these years, they discipled and loved on the people in the places where they worked. While encouraging national pastors to pastor their own churches, they taught individuals to be spiritual leaders in their homes first and then in their church community.

Mom & Dad on his 80th birthday.

While my Dad did not leave much material wealth, our inheritance was growing up in a Christian home. We lived with a mom and dad who loved us and guarded our childhood. Some of my favorite memories are diving into the blue waters of the Caribbean with my dad and our snorkels. More importantly though, he taught me the Scripture as a pastor and a dad.

As the oldest of four children, I walked beside my mother in domestic chores both in our home and in our ministry as missionaries. My youngest brother was born with life-threatening asthma, so he was almost always with me or my mother. Assisting my parents in church-building activities like teaching children in weekly Sunday classes or week long camps, serving in women's ministry and cleaning the church building motivated me to approach cleaning and food jobs with efficiency.

This is my second book related to the home. As I wrote the first book, *Nurturing My Nest*, I felt as though I was dumping out all the ideas that I possessed. The more I wrote the further it seemed that I needed to explain myself. When others read my book, they asked me questions which required lengthy answers about home making. They wondered how I established goals for personal growth. Some asked how I managed the daily, weekly and seasonal cleaning of my home. Others questioned my process of collecting food, organizing my pantry and refrigerator, bulk cooking and freezer cooking. When it comes to the heart behind all this work, my motivation is to strengthen the home and family. My speaking engagements on generous hospitality have been received with the sweetest response. As women I believe there is deep satisfaction in meeting the physical needs of others while serving them in our home. The accumulation of all the rhythms and routines outlined in the following pages cumulated from being raised by an awesome mom and surrounding myself with some of the finest mothers just ahead of me on this journey.

One fall day as I was sitting near my kitchen chatting with a friend in a space we call the morning room. The late afternoon sun teased the colors of a coming vibrant sunset. The air was crisp. The smells of baked bread wafted throughout the house. The unexpected time of conversation for these two busy moms lingered. After several peaceful hours of conversation and coffee drinking, we were close to gathering our children who had been playing enthusiastically in the backyard. Suddenly, she spoke words that still resonate in my mind. She said, "I love to be in your home. It is like there is a hum in your home." I did not understand what she meant. At that moment, I remembered the sound of the dishwasher along with the washer and dryer as she had arrived. I thought that might be the hum that she was referring to at that moment. When I asked her to explain, she stated that while my home seemed clean and orderly, she knew it was not perfect. She knew that the kids had completed their school and contributions earlier in the day. We had hurried because we were excited to enjoy company. Fresh soup and warm bread welcomed them. I chose this meal because it was easy and would feed a hungry crowd of kids. In that moment I thought about how the rhythms and routines created this hum. While it was a simple observation on her part, the loveliness of it made my heart happy.

This thought stayed with me. How I wanted my home to re-flect what she communicated. Being a musical person, I imagined my home full of people who were playing different parts with vari-ous gifts, but living in harmony. I imagined that together we kept a steady rhythm while we worked at our established routines. Only God could orchestrate such balance. But isn't family His idea? As I worked through these routines, I asked for guidance. Beginning with the evaluation of the whole person that God wanted me to be, I con-tinued to pursue God's best for me personally as well as in my home.

One of the deepest questions for all of us to ponder is the examina-tion (exploration) of our purpose. I propose that a woman is naturally inclined to nurturing. Stacey Eldridge in her book "Becoming Myself" states that children get their sense of identity from their fathers and their sense of value or nurturing from their mothers. Regardless of her situation, she desires to nourish and support those she loves. I propose that she embrace that natural enthusiasm that God created within her. If you explore the root of "enthusiasm" in the Latin and Greek, the concept of "God within" is obvious. Processing this information inspires me to remember that my enthusiasm toward the exertion of home making is God's natural giftedness toward nurturing. The ex-ecution of this gift looks different for each person. God did not create us the same. Our strengths and experiences vary. It would be boring if we were identical. Some of us have high energy while others have low energy. I would hate for someone to read this book and feel like they are a failure because they cannot do it all. Start where you are and add patterns you feel fit your goals, your abilities and your energy level.

In the pages of this book, I invite you into my intimate conversations with God about guiding my family to wholeness, into my childhood, my heritage, my musings, my best ideas for a healthy you, my cleaning patterns and my food fetching, my bulk cooking, my nesting, my ideas about easy meals, my passion for serving, my love of home.

Come on in.

Grab your favorite cup of coffee or a yummy hot tea and join me as we explore these simple solutions together. From one homemaker to another, learn how to maximize the routines and rhythms of your home which will stimulate harmony that will bring the hum to your home.

One

HEALTHY YOU

*Teach us to realize the brevity of life, so
that we may grow in wisdom.*

PSALM 90:12 (NLT)

Choosing your BEST LIFE so you can create the "hum" in your home means living your personal best which fuels you to transfer your finest to the work in your home.

Choosing your best life means evaluating all parts of yourself on a regular basis so that you can make necessary changes and improvements. Like the verse above, desire to grow so you will use the briefness of this life wisely. This year I am working on my pilot license, so I am learning to trust the instruments in front of me. Early in this process a fledgling pilot flies only in clear skies where all things can be identified visually. After earning a private pilot's license, a pilot then embarks with courage to earn the instrument rating needed to fly a plane in poor visibility. When competent in this area, a pilot learns to completely trust the instruments in front of him or her to determine where the plane is located and how to keep the wings parallel with the ground.

Life is similar to this concept. In order to know where I am located in life I need to pause and look at the instruments that indicate where the horizon is actually located. Once I am readjusted and definite about my position, I can proceed. In the same way, clarity in functioning to our utmost frees us to live daily with decisions that meet our overall goals. When we fail to center ourselves, we risk wandering aimlessly. When we break down, it is often from fatigue or overload. Sadly, we often give up when we are completely depleted. It is important to restore and replenish ourselves to be able to take care of others well. Just like in an airplane, we must secure our oxygen masks before assisting others with theirs.

Embrace simplicity. Embrace order. Embrace living.

When you find yourself depleted, pause and spend time evaluating all areas of your life. Do you have margin? Do you have space in your days for relaxation? Do you have clarity concerning when to say no to an opportunity? If you find yourself drained, pause and re-evaluate. Limit overstimulation. Consider the source of your exhaus-tion. Identify people and situations that suck the energy out of you. Make changes. Question whether your interactions with others are life giving or life taking.

Exhaustion also sets in when we are too accessible. Choose what is best. Agree to do what you can do well. Build in times of replenishment. Establish a workable way to say "no." When I am asked to do something, I consider if it fits in the goals that I have resolved that best represent my overall mission. If I determine to decline, I respond somewhat like this: "Thank you for demonstrating confidence in me to do this job. However, I feel that this responsibility is worth of a job done well. I am not in a position to give it my very best. Therefore I must forgo the opportunity to say yes. Thank you for honoring me with an invitation to help." The concept is that you say no, but thank them for asking. The result is the same as just simply saying "no," it just sounds friendlier and shows more civility.

Life is somewhat like this idea. If a person always moves forward without pausing to redirect or secure his or her movement, the destination is most uncertain. With your spiritual self as well as your physical and mental self, I recommend looking at the Word of God to be sure that you are on the very best path. Proverbs 3:5,6 (ESV) states that we are to, "Trust in the Lord with all your heart, and do not lean on your own understanding. In all your ways acknowledge him,and he will make straight your paths." Pour over the scriptures for wisdom and direction. As you create a written list of the areas where you would like to hear God, ask Him to speak wisdom to you. Dwell on these concerns for days. Sit quietly and ask God to reveal his very best for you in this season of life and in this area. Ask Him to "create a clean heart" in you. When I am most desperate for God to speak to me, I sit quietly in a peaceful spot, preferably outside, and ask Him to whisper to me. He reveals a secret when he instructs us to "be still and know that I am God." This indicates that if it is noisy in my sphere, I will not be able to hear. This is key to being a mature woman of God who is blessed and living the best life that God planned for me.

Ask what God wants you to do with your time which is actually the time he has given you. In Ecclesiastes 5:5 (NLT) we are reminded that, "It is better to say nothing than to make a promise and not keep it." Don't promise what you will not do or what you cannot do. Commit to completing your work with excellence or don't agree to pledge your time or word. Practically, evaluate all that you are already committed to when considering something new. If your time, skills and willingness fit well, consider responding positively to the request. Resist the urge to agree based on your desire to make the person asking feel warmly toward you. Be thoughtful about your response in conjunction with availability.

Undoubtedly, you have met people who seem vibrant and energized to complete the day ahead. While life offers a number of surprises such as nights that do not allow for sleep and problems that need solving, a healthy attitude to approach each day is important for healthy living. I propose looking deeply at who you are as a whole person. Give God each day. Remember, we can make plans, but God directs our days. Life is predictably unpredictable. Suddenly a kid gets sick or dinner burns or you have an ingredient missing in the meal you planned. For days like this and all days, God knows what is on the schedule. He is never surprised.

Some ask how they can find more time In John 9:4 (NLT) we are reminded that, "We must quickly carry out the tasks assigned us by the one who sent us. The night is coming, and then no one can work." Our life is not infinite. Every day is full of choices of what to do and how to use our time.

So often the focus of our days is trapped in the urgency that propels us to respond to a list of demands. I suggest regularly stepping aside into a quiet contemplative place to consider your whole person. Are you living your best life? This is not a question that asks if your life is perfect. It does not ask if your days are trouble free. It does not ask if you are free from needing to grow.

To live with focus is to live intentionally.

Whether you are a single person, a spouse or a parent, set aside time regularly to evaluate all the parts of yourself. Take a systematic look at all the parts of your life. I suggest evaluating these parts as each season changes or with each transition in life. Examine your situation each spring, summer and fall. Begin with some of these ideas:

Intentional Planning Ahead

I use a tab in the back of my day planner. Since I can add additional tabs, I flip back to early thoughts to encourage myself and thank God for my blessings. Another location for planning might be a journal. If you are a parent, you might contemplate a notebook with a tab for each child in your home. As each season approaches, look at the last page of thoughts. Celebrate progress. Move unmet objectives forward. Dream new desires.

Mikayla with me at a football game.

My middle child did not love "planning sessions" as I aimed to guide her in dreaming her own dreams and methodically working out the details to see them actualized. In high school I would buy a box of ginger snaps if we needed to sort out some details with the planners. Although she loved the bribery, she hated planning. Her first year at college had her scrambling to organize her time on her own. She has asked for a planner for her birthday every year since. This makes me smile. She sees the excitement of laying out your dreams, sorting goals with priorities, and creating an order of phone calls or actions. More is accomplished when you take time to plan.

Invest in a page in your planner or journal that allows you to dream and plan.

Let me illustrate the categories that you would need to consider for your planner:

Physical Health

Do I need to go to the doctor for any concerns or check ups?

Do I need to work on health maintenance?

Am I current on yearly medical tests? blood work? heart? (If necessary, colonoscopy? mammogram? PSA?)

Do I need to schedule a dentist appointment? Teeth cleaning? Orthodontist? Structural work?

Do I need to schedule a vision test? Update my glasses? Contacts?

Do I need to schedule massages? Other wellness appointments?
Chiropractic?

Nutritionist?

Do I need to see a specialist?

If it applies, go over your medications. Make sure you have the
correct dosage. Are you achieving the results you need?

Do I need to seek counseling? How is my mental health?

Am I sleeping well? Am I giving myself enough time to rest?

What do I need to work on to keep myself healthy? Diet changes?
Weight loss?

A curious patient is a healthy patient. Your health is of great importance. Focusing on current needs on a regular basis can propel you to take care of maintenance and neglected concerns. If you are the type of person to google health concerns, ask the doctors you see if there is a site that they can recommend for trustworthy information while you are waiting for your appointment. If you make that a standard question, you may locate several quality sources for data. One question I ask is, "How many patients have you treated with this problem?" Experience is a critical feature that secures the most competent solution. Another question might be "What would you do if this was your issue?" or "What would you do if this was your wife's medical concern?" or "Can I treat this another way? Can I treat this nutritionally?"

Be sure to develop a written list of concerns when anticipating a doctor's appointment. Sometimes when you are in an appointment, you forget a critical concern. A list prevents this lapse. Be honest with your health issues. Be proactive and not reactive. Making significant changes in lifestyle takes, first of all, mental strength. Most of this requires planning and preparation. Frankly, staying healthy and moving toward a better place with my health requires mental resolve. For me, I imagine the place that I will be in if I don't make needed changes.

Many doctors will respond to any issues that prompted the visit, but some will not discuss preventative ideas unless asked. Many patients just want a prescription, not a conversation about how to prevent the problem.

If you have an ongoing issue, ask if there is anything you can do to completely heal it. Or what is the best way to maintain a healthy lifestyle if it is a permanent problem? Since I have had eleven pregnancies, I struggle with swollen legs when I travel and even just driving around town transporting kids on a long day. This is an continuing problem. Since I love to travel and am frequently taking my children to speech and debate competitions, this needs to be addressed. So, I continue to search for a solution. In hope of new information, I often include this concern in a routine doctor's appointment. I certainly do not want to have mobility issues because my veins in my legs could be fixed, but I failed to ask the right person.

As believers in Christ Jesus, we rest assured that God created us in the glorious image of Himself. I believe that since God dwells within us, we are called to honor the body as His temple. Our bodies are worthy of care. It is through our bodies that we engage in all that God intends for us in this world. Engage in wholeness. The healthier our bodies are, the more intensely we detect the goodness of the world around us.

Pursuing a pattern of work and rest respects our humanity. Honoring the Sabbath in some form is simple obedience to God's order of nature. Recognizing the limits of our humanness is a must. Rest invites relaxation, refreshment and replenishment. I am finite. I must live within the boundaries of my human potential. My body is made for rest.

Be empowered with working knowledge of your medical needs. Pursue healthy choices so that you live your best life.

Sabbaticals

Consider a sabbatical after pushing through an event or a trip or any busy season. Take a sabbatical following sickness, death of a loved one, caregiving, loss or any major stressor. Several of my friends laugh when I say this, but I always mean it when I tell them that I am going to take a sabbatical. Often when returning from competition, a trip or an intense amount of responsibility, I declare that I am going to take a sabbatical. This means that I am going to hibernate with my family. No screen time. Limited communication via text. No email. No social media. No leaving the house. Long baths or showers. Self care such as mud masks, lots of lotion and protein drinks. Fresh fruit and vegetables. Home all day. Long walks. Naps. Time for uninterrupted conversations. Emptying suitcases. Laundry. Cleaning our home. Setting things in order. Cleaning out the refrigerator. Fresh food for the time ahead. Spending long periods with our Bibles and prayer. SLEEP! Lots of cuddle time. Think relaxation, refreshment and replenishment.

Sophie bear loves to cuddle.

Spiritual Health

Some of the questions that I pose to myself when evaluating my spiritual life:

Am I reading my Bible daily and studying intensely in one area?

Am I participating in a community of believers studying the Bible?

Am I praying? Intentionally? Am I growing in my prayer life?

Am I serving?

Am I practicing hospitality?

Am I giving to my local church? To missions?

Am I serving in my Christian community and outside of my church?

Am I ministering to my family spiritually? Extended family?

Am I investing time in discipling someone else? A group?

Am I memorizing scripture?

Am I trusting Christ to live His life through me?

Am I resting in His peace?'

Since God gave me children, I take my responsibility to train them spiritually very seriously. As I consider what I need to learn, I also evaluate whether I am teaching them what is essential for them to study. My personal spiritual journey began when I was just a young girl. My parents independently determined that they wanted to invest their lives in sharing the love of Jesus with unreached people groups. So, when they met in college they found each other and decided to team up. My early years were spent on a remote island in the West Indies called St. Lucia. Each morning my mother would rise and turn on the gas stove to boil the sizable pots of water which were waiting. All water used for drinking and any cooking had to be boiled. Then she would slip off into the nearby patio and spend thirty minutes to an hour with God. Many times she would not know that I had followed her. I would listen quietly nearby as she would pray out loud. Just watching her daily apply the scripture to her life and knowing how intensely she conversed with God was ingrained in my soul. Her example inspired me to embrace a life of loving God.

All of us are more convinced by actions than words. I ask myself, "Am I living in a way that persuades others, in particular my family, to grasp the truths and blessing of life lived to love God? What do my children see in me that draws them to a lifestyle of consistent, daily growing in spiritual disciplines?" When I refer to spiritual disciplines, I mean reading the Bible daily, studying deeply on a regular basis, praying, sharing with others, hospitality and doing service outside my home.

Relational Health

Ask yourself who you are. What roles do you play?

I am a woman.
I am a wife.
I am a mother.
I am a mother-in-law.
I am a sister-in-law.
I am a daughter.
I am a sister.
I am an aunt.
I am a teacher.
I am a friend.

I am a neighbor.
I am a group leader.
I am a caregiver.
I am a mentor.
I am a grandmother.
I am a boss.
I am a leader.

Family walk.

List the roles you play. Ask yourself if are forgetting your responsibilities or influence in any of these places. Be intentional. If you need to, take your planner and think through the opportunities that you have to make an impact on those in your path. Evaluate. Plan. Do.

"Wise people think before they act; fools don't--and even brag about their foolishness" (Proverbs 13:16 NLT)." Choose wisdom. Plan, then act intentionally. It has been said that if you fail to plan, you plan to fail. Some even believe that if you aim at nothing, you will hit it.

You may need to mark your calendar and make a call or do lunch on a regular basis. For me, my planner functions as my brain. Some use a digital system while others choose a paper based plan. Mine is paper. Once you determine your goals, put them into your system so that you will not forget to act on maintaining and developing the relationships in your life.

Mental Health

Ask if you are challenging yourself with mentally stimulating material.

What books are you reading? Or podcasts?
Have I incorporated self-care time?
What do I do with my free time?
Does my entertainment grow me?
Do I use much of my down time to travel time or grow?
Am I avoiding negativity in my life?
What am I trying to learn?

While it is awesome to play music, consider growing by listening to audio books or listening to podcasts in the car or while waiting.

Be thoughtful about what you read. Prioritize spiritual disciplines. Methodically, study the Word of God. This is the most important book you can study. Choose a book of the Bible to read over and over while studying it inductively. Work through weekly Bible studies in community at your church. Attend a Kay Arthur study or do one on your own at home. Stay involved in your local church, and in the women's ministry. Take a Bible study together with others in your church community. Locate a quality source for online study such as John Piper. Discipline your time. II Timothy 2:15 (NLT) reminds us to "Work hard so you can present yourself to God and receive his approval. Be a good worker, one who does not need to be ashamed and who correctly explains the word of truth." Be educated. Be a learner. Be a seeker. If reading is challenging for you, embark on a plan to consume God's Word with an audible source. Knowing God is a lifetime journey.

Select books that grow you in spiritual ways, self-improvement, biographical sketches, skills, your career field and healthy fiction. This past year I have read two books on self-improvement, three cookbooks, a book on hospitality, another Jan Karon book, a true life story about an orphan, two biographies, numerous educational resource books along with a myriad of spiritual improvement books. Maintaining a clutter free home helps with mental health.

Other ideas for creating your best self mentally are to do crossword puzzles, play bridge and work Sudoku. Plan to be mentally healthy by working your brain. Many of us recognize how exercising our bodies is beneficial. In the same way, purposeful action mentally keeps us sharp.

Emotional Health

Question if you are balanced emotionally. What is your emotional IQ? If you have any unsolved business with someone, if you are finding yourself repeating conflicts with someone you love, if you are struggling to move forward, it might be worth going to see a counselor. A truly confidential friend might also be a great option. Spend time considering these questions:

Am I interacting in a healthy way with my family?
Do my emotions fluctuate? What can I do to be more balanced?
Do I need to seek forgiveness?
Do I need to give forgiveness even if I am not asked?
(Bitterness will not punish the wrongdoer, but it will hurt me.)
Do I need to pay back a debt? Focus on retribution.
Am I even tempered? If not, why not?

Pray for sensitivity to respond to anything that needs to change or adjust. "In all your ways acknowledge him, and he will make straight your paths" (Proverbs 3:6 ESV). This passage clearly directs me to seek God's wisdom."

One of the questions above was, "Am I even tempered?" It is important to work toward being stable emotionally. If I am not, I ask myself, "what needs to be done so that I am not emotionally needy?" What can I do to help myself not be emotionally drained or emotionally draining on those with whom I interact with every day? Sometime my emotions are affected by female problems or lack of proper food and sleep. Explore the cause and work toward a solution. Don't be afraid to ask those who love you most how they would answer this question about you.

This goes back to asking yourself about your physical condition. You may need to go for medical testing. You may need to add or subtract medication. The struggle may be related to a need for more nutrient dense foods. Regular exercise or different food can make all the difference. While I do not have any pressing health concerns, I am working toward more physical exercise on a daily basis.

When reading *Sacred Rhythms* by Ruth Haley Barton, this list described some spiritual disciplines that correspond to our needs. Read through it and notice any helpful suggestions.

Sins and Negative Patterns	**Corresponding Disciplines**
Gossip/sins of speech	Silence, self-examination
Anxiety and worry	Breath prayer, Scripture reflection
Envy and competitiveness	Solitude, self-examination
Discontent	Attending to desire
Self-reliance	Silence, prayer, community
Avoidance patterns	Community, spiritual friendship
Over-busyness	Solitude, discernment, sabbath
Anger and bitterness	Silence, self-examination, confession
Feelings of inadequacy	Examen of consciousness, self-knowledge and Celebration
Guilt, shame	Solitude, confession, forgiveness
Lust	Attending to desire in God's presence
Restlessness or stress	Solitude, silence, breath prayer
Lethargy and/or laziness	Caring for the body, exercise
Lack of faith	Prayer, Scripture
Feelings of isolation	Examen of consciousness, community
Selfishness and self-centeredness	Prayer and worship in community
Lack of direction	Discernment, listening to the body

Aim for progress, not perfection, in maintaining a healthy body, cultivating spiritual growth, maturing relationships, expanding mentally and thriving emotionally.

Celebrate Progress

Set aside time periodically to evaluate yourself as a whole person. Consider evaluations at the beginning of each season. Perhaps you could assess yourself in January, May and September. These are the times where our schedule makes adjustments. Work toward self-evaluation at least twice a year.

Motivating Walls

Bible Verses

Some other thoughts about creating healthy living for the whole person involve strategically placing scripture verses throughout your living space. My favorite location for scripture is in the bathroom across from the toilet. While this seems a little bit funny to say, I am positive that it works well in accomplishing my goals. My intention is to encourage frequent reading of the scripture. When placing scripture in an area with continual viewing, it is quickly memorized. The location promotes meditation. Just saying. While I prefer Bible verses, I also post quality quotes and motivation in critical locations throughout our home.

Outside of photos I purposely hang as many Bible verses on my walls as I can possibly fit. While I have seen many raised eyebrows at this suggestion, I firmly believe that the best place to post scripture in any home is directly across from the toilet. Really, most occupants of the seat nearby will look at these words and read them. They have time. One of the little girls that grew up at my house instantly memorized any verse that I posted anywhere in the house. To this day, she rattles them off perfectly. This is a true testament to a successful idea. Try it.

Photos

One of the conflicts for me concerning wall space is whether to desire wall space or windows. The struggle is real. Photos of family are most important as they are a sort of visual history. Photos bring family that is grown or not alive back to us as clearly as the day that lives eternally in the photo. Photos build relationships such as the marriage bond. Photos remind us of the happy times in our journey. Here is a picture of my handsome sons followed by one of my pretty girls.

The boys.

The girls.

Look for wall spaces to post the history of your adventures. Print pictures of your immediate family as well as your extended family. Play the historian. What does your home communicate about you? Is it full of decorations or photos of those you love? Clearly, I value pictures of the faces that are dearest to me as well as photos that mark moments in my story. I want to celebrate people. That is why I love taking pictures. That is why I love posting pictures. That is why I love celebrating the stories behind the people.

Messages

Other items covering our walls and in frames might include meaning-ful quotes. We also praise hard work, so we look for ways to display awards and meaningful accomplishments.

~

Conclusion

Being a WHOLE person means living my best life by walking slowly enough to be in the moments of my life. As a planner and a doer, I purpose to BE in the moments. I often repeat to myself, "Wherever you are, BE all there." It is so easy to be somewhere physically but not there in my whole self. I am working on being present.

One of my favorite passages in 2 Peter 1:5-8 reminds me of what I must do to avoid being ineffective and unfruitful. God calls me to make a diligent effort to supplement my position as a child of God by pursuing virtue, knowledge, self-control, consistency, God-likeness, brotherly affection, and love.

In being attentive to the fragility of life, I contemplate my life. Have I lived today well? Have I done today the things that God or-dained for me to do? Last year I waited with my mother in her home as my father lived the last days of his life. Those remaining days of his life were unbelievably exhausting. When I say that they were the eternal night, I speak truth. I was up all day doing the things that the day de-manded, but at night I stayed with my dad so my mother could sleep. She had been caring for my dad for two years in his cancer journey.

If you know a caregiver, stop right now and call them. Write them a note. Always look for ways to lighten their load. Give them hugs whenever you can reach them physically. They are living in a tunnel. They are so very tired. They are in great need of our attentiveness.

For two weeks I stayed awake almost around the clock. Every morning, my mother and I sat together and ate breakfast. My favorite breakfast was avocados on toast with fried eggs. We would make a list of what we needed to do that day. My Godly mother would not pray what I might pray. I might have asked God to help us to be productive. I might have prayed that God help us to complete all the things on this list. What did she pray? She prayed that our day would be filled with all that He (God) intended for our day. Sometimes our day was completed with much of what we suspected was "needed." Other days left much on the list undone. We did not have many more days with Dad.

We sat. We read scripture. We prayed out loud. The family came and we did church that final Sunday morning. It seemed a holy place with all of us gathered like a tight band around the unfamiliar hospital bed in my parents' room. In addition to fine hymns, one of dad's loves had always been Irish music. In those final days we played every Ronan Tynan song for hours. The grandeur of his rendition of *Amazing Grace* paired with *Going Home* brings me to tears just thinking about it.

I re-learned something very important on those days. Each day I should be mindful of what God wants for my day. Sometimes my day needs to be ordered with high levels of productivity. Other days I need to study or serve or just rest. Honor the rhythm of life by balancing work and rest.

When we think of a home, we imagine the interior as the rooms and their furnishings. Perhaps the real interior of our home is the inside of us. Consider the truth that a mother sets the tone of the home. To meet this challenge well, regularly review all the parts of who you are. Determine to be the healthiest version of yourself. Be a healthy you!

Life is a series of changes and variation. God created variety. Embrace change. While making plans is helpful, my willingness to be spontaneous, to prioritize people and to choose what is best will result in my living my best life.

Two

Cleaning - Home Maintenance

Never be lazy, but work hard and
serve the Lord enthusiastically.

Romans 12:11 NLT

Some of us love the process of cleaning just as much as we enjoy the results. Others struggle with the patterns necessary to
maintain their living space daily, weekly and seasonally. In order to
live this life well, we must create a plan to maintain our space. Let's be
honest, maintaining a home is hard work. When we are in the grind
and feel like maids while doing all the house jobs, pause. Remember
this verse in Romans 12 that encourages us to serve our family and
others who enter our home as we would serve the Lord. Work enthusiastically with our minds toward honoring God. How would I wait
on Jesus Christ if he were the guest in my home? How can I treat
my family in a manner that reflects my effort to be hospitable as if I
am hosting my Savior? It takes some thinking, but this truth often
changes my attitude toward the management of my home. God has

given me this amazing opportunity to keep a home, love a family and honor him with a generous spirit. This section is about rhythms and routines that offer workable patterns which can be personalized to meet your needs. The big idea behind purging and deep cleaning is to create a livable space that is relatively simple to maintain on a daily and weekly basis. Sometimes we have the help of a spouse and sometimes we don't. Ideally, teamwork is best. Do what works best for you.

As homemakers, cleaning is part of our responsibility. It is also our responsibility to train the next generation to cook and to maintain the spaces where they live. Since we will invest many years in cleaning and maintaining, it is worth our time to develop patterns that create the most pleasant, livable space. As with any skill, observe others who are successful, educate yourself on workable patterns and read about how the job is done well. Adapt what you learn to your needs and lifestyle. Start where you are now and develop patterns that win for you. Remember, progress, not perfection!

In college, waitressing and cleaning houses paid the entirety of my bill. I graduated debt free. In providing a cleaning service in other's homes as an independent contractor, efficient patterns sped up the process. Most homes were given a general cleaning in 3-4 hours weekly working alone. The expertise that comes from just doing the work repeatedly tested patterns of speed and efficiency.

Determine what works best for you. Customize your patterns. Identify your schedule. Modify your routines.

When I read Proverbs 31:27, "She carefully watches everything in her household and suffers nothing from laziness," I am reminded of my desire to maintain order with the space that is my responsibility. While it may be a small space or a sizable area, it is mine to maintain.

Let's start with daily and weekly cleaning and then look at the seasonal cleaning and purging.

Cleaning - Couples without Children

DAILY AND WEEKLY

In early marriage my husband and I both worked nearly 50 hours a week. Since we shared the financial responsibility of our team, we listed all of the responsibilities related to our home and car. Once we estimated the time involved in these tasks, we divided them between us. Currently, we still have children at home, but we will soon be working toward keeping a home again with just the two of us. The key is to make a list together of what you think needs to be done. If you designate the time needed for each task, that helps. Lastly, determine who will do the assignment.

DAILY

Empty trash in kitchen
Empty dishwasher
Make beds
Pick up/Put away
20-30 minutes from the weekly maintenance jobs list.

WEEKLY
LEAH
Wash clothes (Look to the end of this chapter for a section on laundry)
Change sheets & towels
Iron clothes
Clean bathrooms
Dust
Vacuum, Sweep and Mop floors
Food planning/Grocery shopping
Meals
Keep flower beds weeded/mulched (in season)

TIM
Drop off and pick up dry cleaning (mostly his)
Vacuum and wash both cars (this was "BC" - before children)
Vacuum whole house
Collect trash throughout house and paper shredder
Help with meal clean-up
Mow/weed eat/leaf blow (in season)

Below is how we sorted these responsibilities into days.

Monday: wash clothes, change sheets and towels, sweep outside front and back doors/patio, iron

Tuesday: clean bathrooms (showers, toilets, sinks, mirrors, floors)

Wednesday: straighten, pick up and put away, dust

Thursday: vacuum whole house (including stairs), mop all floors in kitchen, bathroom and patio areas.

Friday: Fun Friday. Finish anything that did not get done during the week. Do a deep cleaning project. Or just run errands and have fun with a friend.

Saturday: outside responsibilities together, meal plan, shop for food

Sunday: worship at church together. Spend time with family and friends. Rest. Enjoy having friends and family for a meal and conversation. Food preparation for the week.

Much of the cleaning could be done on one day if that works better. For years, we would clean on Thursday afternoons. Do what works best for you and your schedule!

Cleaning With Children

DAILY AND WEEKLY

Some parents express that children should not be responsible for housework. I do not hold to this theory. Here are some questions to ask yourself when deciding about cleaning responsibilities as they relate to your children. Were you ready to independently take on cleaning responsibilities once you left your parents' home? Were you ready to care for your living space when you moved out on your own? If so, how did you mature in those skills? If not, what did you have to learn as an adult? Were you prepared to clean and cook? Did you already practice routines that led to rhythms of making your home?

I propose that each child should be raised to do all skills needed for adult life. Some of this preparation requires maintaining your space and completing the work listed above. Children are capable of contributing to the family. Expect them to help for the benefit of the rest of the family. This section includes an age-appropriate contribution list.

This enables proper expectations. Most are surprised to read over this list and discover what their child is capable of at their age. Just for clarification, I resist using the word "chore" which conjures up an inaudible sigh. Instead, we select "contribution" which promotes teamwork. I contend that young ones who buy into this notion of playing team with the family will also think about marriage like a team.

> *"Give instruction to a wise man, and he*
> *will be still wiser; teach a righteous man,*
> *and he will increase in learning."*

PROVERBS 9:9 ESV

Contribution Chart

PERSONAL CONTRIBUTIONS
(First thing EVERY morning before breakfast)
Note: Giving each child an alarm clock helps with this process.
Personal:
Make bed
Brush teeth
Brush Hair
Dress
God & I time

Family Contributions

Note: Distribute these tasks appropriately between children based on age and ability. Rotate these jobs each season. We rotate jobs in January, June and August. Initiate the "Expect and Inspect" concept so that your children will learn to do the job correctly, and you will not be overly frustrated. This means that you have to focus on teaching the contribution to each child during this time. Don't just assign it and go off to take care of something on your list. In fact, expect to follow each child with your hands behind your back directing the steps of the job. This is time consuming for awhile. Don't expect perfection. Expect it won't be done perfectly. Be okay to live with imperfection. It will get better in time, and they will be an asset without adding to your workload.

Empty dishwasher

Wipe down all kitchen counters

Pets - Fresh water, food, brush, pet, kiss and snuggle

(Yes, that is what I said. Those fur babies are just ready for love.)

Sweep or vacuum floors (This usually means main living spaces such as kitchen, breakfast area and living room. The focus here is daily maintenance of high traffic areas.)

Mom's helper (check rooms, bathrooms, runner)

A runner is someone that puts things away in the correct location. Select this person carefully. If your child has ADHD, the distractibility will drive you crazy. My best runner was my youngest boy for years. He never got "lost." Moms, you know what I mean. Have you ever handed an item to a child to deliver to a location only to have them come back and ask you where the item in their hand was supposed to go? You can't make this stuff up.

Weekly (2-3 hours)

List each family member and an age-appropriate list for them. This will change twice a year as each child masters new skills and moves on to new ones. If they know they will keep chores they don't master, it might encourage them to complete them correctly.

Outside of contributions, select some jobs which allow your child to earn money. Remember your child will grow to be an adult. Many of their habits as adults will result from money patterns they learn as they develop. Developing a strong work ethic is key to success. Remember that these bonus jobs need to be taught and checked too. Each family needs to sort out what is a contribution and what needs to be earned. Don't pay your child more for a bonus job than others might. This creates unrealistic expectations. One girl that I knew would ride the riding lawn mower for two acres. She did not weed eat or blow. She was paid $200 each time she completed this activity. Most people will not replicate this experience. She may be frustrated when someone later wants to pay her the standard amount. These may also be the kids who do gain work experience as teens.

Bonus Jobs Ideas

Babysit - earnings depending on the number of kids and the length of time
Pet sit (varies)
Dog walk
Wash a vehicle (inside and outside)
Organize a garage, or shed or closet
Mother's helper - Help a mom with small children. Assist with the children and do any jobs that she needs to have done. The mom is typically home when you are helping. Sometimes she might want you to watch the children while she cleans house.
Spring cleaning jobs such as washing all the garbage cans
Washing bedding, cleaning windows
Weeding in flower beds
Lifeguard duties

Help a senior
Tutor kids in your favorite subject.
Grade papers
Boat or camper cleaning
House sit/water plants/bring in mail

Mom - Supervise

Remember to expect quality work and inspect a finished job.
If possible, parent cleans parent bedroom, bathroom and declutters.
Putting things away on a regular basis is work that requires discipline,
but it is what keeps order. Give yourself grace when you are exhausted.

Make a list of the needed jobs for your home and sort them out
based on the number of children and their abilities. Personalize this
concept for your family and space.

You may continue the process with your own jobs once the kids finish and you have inspected their work. Once you practice this system for
a while, patience will win out. Your children will surprise you and slip
into the flow of the work. For those children who tend to always resist
work, be patient and keep plugging away. Don't quit. Don't be discour-
aged. Even if they never embrace the system that you create, they will be
progressing in their skills. Remember, progress not perfection.

"She is energetic and strong, a hard worker" (Proverbs 31:17 NLT).
Communicate the value of hard work which leads to a job well done.

Note: Whoever is cleaning a living space, such as a bathroom, is responsible for restocking it. For instance, the bathroom may need more
toilet paper or hand soap.

My messiest child was most definitely my oldest. He participated in the above process, but really struggled to maintain his own space. This boy would panic when Katie (child number two) and I would lock ourselves in his room with garbage bags and start cleaning. Usually, the floor was not visible. First, we grabbed up all the paper and empty packaging. Then we located all clothes and shoes determining whether they needed to be put away or washed. While he was my oldest and first "project," he experienced delayed maturity in this area. He was an excessive reader whose first ACT was a 33, so we can celebrate those things. Update: He is now 26 and is embracing cleanliness. As a single, young man, he is living minimally. This month, he bought a new vacuum cleaner and mop. Just this week, he called and asked me to help him pick out a rug for his entrance to keep less dirt from coming into his living space. Miracles never cease!

T.J. and Riley.

Individual letters on this list represent the names of my children. The numbers are their ages. This is a sample chart. Insert the names of your children. This list was created with four of my children. My oldest had already gone to college.

Sample Weekly Contribution Chart:

K (15) laundry
ironing
plan food prep, purchasing & cooking
straighten pantry
M (13) downstairs bathroom kid's bathroom
sweep & mop all 1st floor
clean glass on all outer doors
litter box
J (11) dust 1st floor,
vacuum 2nd floor
straighten & vacuum school room
shoe basket
clean & vacuum one vehicle
J (9) straighten & wipe out refrigerator, straighten pantry
vacuum stairs
collect garbage throughout the whole house
sweep outside front door
sweep back steps and back door

Age Appropriate Contributions
ages 2-3
make their bed with help

pick up toys with supervision
put dirty clothes in laundry chute or basket
put clean water in pet dish
food in pet dish
brush pets
dust with a mitt

age 4-5
get dressed with minimal help
bring own things from car
help unload groceries
set the table
help with some food preparation
match socks
fold washcloths and hand towels
hang towel on hook in bathroom
wipe off bathroom sink
wipe off kitchen table

age 6-7
make bed every day
brush teeth (with timer)
comb hair
dress
write thank you notes
supervised vacuum own room
vacuum other rooms
fold laundry with help
empty dishwasher with help
prepare food with help
empty trash cans throughout the house

age 8-11
personal hygiene
work toward independent routines
clean bedroom
school work
keep up with own items
wake up with alarm clock independently
wash dishes, dry and put away
wash family car inside and out with help, complete easy meals alone
clean a bathroom with help
put all clean clothes away

ages 12-13
all personal hygiene
all personal belongings
all school related work
keep own room tidy
vacuum and dust own room
set alarm and wake independently to alarm
write invitations and thank you notes
change sheets
change light bulbs
change vacuum bag
dust
vacuum
clean bathroom
clean dishes
wipe surfaces in kitchen
clean mirrors
mow with help

age 14-15
all personal hygiene
maintain personal space, property and clothes (wash, dry, iron and put away)
library checkout and return
all school work
all yard work
prepare grocery list and shop with supervision
prepare one family meal a week
wash windows
participate in seasonal cleaning

ages 16-18
all above
earn money
spend money responsibly
open checking account and use with supervision
purchase clothes
(Determine a clothing budget. Create a need list after cleaning through clothes for that season. Shop for needs with budget.)
Responsible for maintenance for any car they drive
(gas, oil changes, tire pressure, car wash, vacuum)
all yard work
all house work
deep cleaning household appliances
deep cleaning the garage and attic
deep cleaning closets

READY to launch into adult life.

Expect and Inspect Method

One last note about children and cleaning. Consider putting up a new chart on January first and in the beginning of summer. As the family launches into a new season, encourage each person that they are going to learn a new job. State that you want them to be efficient in all areas. (Anticipate moans here. It is what it is.) When initiating a new job, spend time demonstrating the task. Stand back, putting your hands behind your back while watching your child do the new job. Direct with your words. Be sure to speak life giving (encouraging) words as you guide verbally. Do this with each child for new tasks. Week two might require this same supervision with hands behind the back and orally directing. By week three you should be able to assign the duty and just inspect to ensure the job was completed correctly.

Let me pause here and state that some kids will master these tasks more quickly than others. Some are naturally organized and enjoy sorting. Others will struggle to complete these tasks because they are not interested or because the skill is more challenging for them. Some will never ever complete the job to your satisfaction. With five children, I readily admit that some of mine left their rooms a disaster when they moved out. My job was to train them and I feel that I did my best. Some required more than two weeks of close supervision. Always keep in mind that your end goal is to raise a competent adult. Keeping our living space clean is really essential for all of us. Some struggle with certain tasks because of their individual limitations. Don't lose hope. It is a journey. Do your best. Ask your child to do their best.

Some of mine needed extra encouragement to reach a standard of excellence. When met with continued resistance, remind the child that this job will be theirs until they demonstrate mastery. Such prodding proved successful for some. Remember that you may have a child that resists all the time, forever. They still need to know all that you are trying to teach them. Believe it or not, your stubborn child is paying attention and may do the task perfectly later when you are not watching. Consider what motivates this young person. Pray about your response. Taking something that they love away or delaying an activity may urge them to progress. Praise them for their efforts and progress. Part of our job as parents is to train them in all ways for the future. Keep the end goal in mind.

⌒⟩

Cleaning - living alone

DAILY AND WEEKLY
Consider the tasks that are important to you in maintaining your home and vehicle. This is a system that I believe works well.

DAILY
Empty trash in kitchen
Empty dishwasher
Make bed
Pick up/put away
20 minutes of maintenance (See maintenance section)

WEEKLY
Wash clothes
Change sheets & towels
Iron clothes
Drop and pick up dry cleaning
Declutter, put away
Clean bathrooms
Dust

Vacuum whole house
Mop floors
Food planning/Grocery shopping
Meals/Food prep
Yard work
Mow/Blow leaves/Weed eating
Keep flower beds weeded/mulched (seasonal)
Vacuum and wash car
Collect trash throughout house and paper shredder

In order to maintain your home each week, either choose jobs from a daily list or push all of the work into a two hour window once a week. This option may change as your schedule adjusts. Do what works for you. Here is an idea of how you might sort the responsibilities into smaller time sections over the week.

Monday: wash clothes, change sheets and towels, clean entrances, sweep under rugs, clean glass in doors, sweep all steps inside and outside the house
Tuesday: clean bathrooms (showers, toilets, sinks, mirrors, floors),restock paper products throughout the house
Wednesday: straighten, pick up and put away, dust
Thursday: vacuum whole house (including stairs)
Friday: (Fun Friday) Complete unfinished jobs that did not get done during the week. Do a deep cleaning project. Run errands. Have lunch with a friend.
Saturday: outside responsibilities
Sunday: worship at church. spend time with family and friends. Rest. Enjoy friends and family for a meal and conversation. Practice hospitality.

Much of the cleaning could be done on one day if that works better. For years, we would clean on Thursday afternoons for two hours. Don't get bogged down in one area. Keep the big picture the focus. Save deep cleaning for a day on its own.

Do what works best for you!

Speed Cleaning regularly

Start with a cup of coffee-just kidding. If you keep the pace of daily contributions and the once a week cleaning, there will still remain a need for seasonal cleaning, deep cleaning and purging. If your schedule allows, select a time weekly for ongoing maintenance. Find at least 30 minutes (daily or weekly?) to focus on one of the trouble areas in your home. Perhaps you want to work through cleaning your kitchen. Once you have the 30 minutes to speed clean, set the timer for 30 minutes. Determine that you will focus on the task and not let anything interrupt. Begin by taking the drawer's contents out and laying them on a towel on the counter. Vacuum and wipe out the drawer and any sorting boxes you plan to reuse in the drawer. Sort the contents by the Trash, Donate, Keep method. I really appreciate Marie Kondo's method of only keeping an item that sparks joy. It helps to let go of an item using that concept. Once the trash and donations are separated out, reorganize the items you plan to keep. Keeping an eye on the timer, your decisions will need to be made quickly. By focusing solely on the job, racing the clock and finishing a small job completely, you will gain continued confidence for your next endeavor.

Once you implement speed cleaning into your weekly schedule, you will be surprised how much will be accomplished around your house. You might even be motivated to do speed cleaning with larger areas and for longer periods of time.

⁓

Monthly Cleaning

Each week add one additional cleaning task to your list in order to maintain the rhythm of clean in your home. In college I cleaned houses to pay for my tuition. By adding one of the jobs below to each week, these spaces were cleaned once a month. It is an idea that works well for maintenance of frequently used areas.

> week 1: clean your oven, change filters in home, change fire alarm batteries
> week 2: clean freezer and refrigerator
> week 3: ironing, mending, locate cobwebs
> week 4: baseboards, window sills

⁓

One Day Seasonal Cleaning

Make a list of the areas in your home. Evaluate the greatest needs based on the time you have available. Create a realistic list. Plan to not prepare food as you will be working on cleaning instead of doing any cooking that day. Plan to order pizza or buy it ready to go. (We are fresh food snobs, so we LOVE Papa Murphy's made ready to cook pizzas.)

Gather all the tools you need to be successful (see list further in this chapter).

Select a day where you have no anticipated interruptions along with a large cup of coffee--just kidding. (Not kidding.)

Start early. Don't stop until all areas have been put away completely.

Leave no evidence that there is a job in progress. Celebrate a successful day of work. Do not allow yourself to be bogged down with detailed work on one area unless that is how you decided to spend the day.

If you only have one day, focus on overall straightening and putting away. This would involve the sorting mentioned in this chapter that includes the trash, donate and keep method. If keeping, remember that it needs to be put away before you finish for the day. Depending on where you are on your weekly cleaning, start with basic cleaning. Then, select from the off-season cleaning list the items that seem most urgent.

Another idea on how to do seasonal cleaning is to select one category, one section of your house or just one room to tackle. List your goals. I do a great deal of thinking about how I am going to clean before I begin. This really speeds up the process. Identify the categories in the space. Consider how you want to use the space. Recognize the storage availability and furniture in this room. If you mentally work through the cleaning and storage in a space before you start the job, your work will contain less hiccups.

A fun idea regarding your one day cleaning spree is to ask a friend if she would join you in exchange for joining her in cleaning her home in one day. If you don't have a friend who has comparable speed and standards, consider hiring someone to assist on that day.

Since we are active in our church community, we embrace mission efforts. We go ourselves and we send people by helping them financially. Whether it is a project near or far, it usually requires funds. When we go, we aim to work for our trip. As I write this book, my youngest son, Joseph, is earning money to return for the third time to Columbia, South America. He has fallen in love with so many of the children in the orphanage where he serves. He is working by moving furniture, power washing and doing yard work in exchange for donations to his trip. When you are needing an extra hand, call your church office and ask if anyone is needing assistance for an upcoming trip. Invite them to be part of your cleaning efforts in exchange for financial support for their mission trip. This sort of swap is a serious win for all.

⌒

Seasonal Cleaning - Going deep (with or without kids)

If you live in any space, it will require regular maintenance. When you take some time regularly to tackle the upkeep of your living area, it should not become overwhelming. Many books are written on cleaning. This is certainly not the one and only way to manage your stuff. My ideas are an accumulated from being on this path for a long time as well as from reading numerous books on organizing and cleaning. Early on, I cleaned houses to pay for much of my college costs. Years of experience forced me to be efficient. These ideas work for me.

Let's face it, clutter is an ongoing challenge. Each day things are coming into your home. If you pay attention to what is going in and out, you might conclude that more is coming in. Most would agree that this is true.

Do not run out and buy organizing containers. Buying baskets, bins and holders is not the way to begin. If organizing tools are necessary, they should be purchased at the end of the cleaning process once the exact needs are clear and measurements are taken. If the costs of buying organizers has held you back, be free. You should start without them.

Some refer to this 2-3 times a year of cleaning as spring cleaning. I notice that deep cleaning occurs right after Christmas, as well as in the spring and fall when the temperatures change. Often clothes are moved around. Furniture and decor adjusts as the weather presents new expectations.

When you get excited about cleaning because the air is crisp, or if it is because moving things around reveals a need to clean, just begin. Do it right away. Most of maintenance around the home is in your mind. When the mood strikes, go with it.

LOCATE YOUR TOOLS
dusting cloths
> Note: My favorite are Norwex cleaning cloths and polishing cloths. They do an excellent job with just hot water. I also love old t-shirts and old kitchen towels especially for dirty jobs that dictate the cloth be thrown away when the job is complete.

pail for water
vinegar (white)
rubber gloves
old toothbrush
paper towels
Windex
mop
vac for stairs
vac for floors
Mr. Clean eraser

METHODS TO TRY
One room at a time. Be thorough. This is spring cleaning. Don't hurry. Choose one type of area to clean. For example, work through clothes throughout the house. Or just clean the communal living spaces. List jobs that need to be completed. Delegate to helpers. (This is another "expect and inspect" situation.)

Work hard during designated time and then plan an outing or fun food as a reward.

Time yourself. Race the timer.

WHAT NEEDS TO BE CLEANED IN SPRING CLEANING?

closets

all cabinets

kitchen cabinets

clean refrigerator

clean freezer

clean stovetop

toss expired food in refrigerator/freezer/pantry

toss expired medicine

resort silverware drawers, vac out

restock all paper products

wash all bedding

wash pillows

wash comforters or dry clean

change out seasonal clothing

donate clothing

bathroom cabinets

clean shower head

wipe/vacuum bathroom vents

vacuum heating and air vents and change out filters

vacuum walls

wash all rugs

toss expired beauty products

steam clean all carpets

clean the interior of inside and outside garbage cans

deep clean bathrooms (walls of bathroom, walls of shower, garbage can, shower doors, light fixtures, bathroom fan)

clean all glass on doors and mirrors
light fixtures
blinds
dust, polish, oil furniture
upholstered furniture - steam cleaned, brushed, vacuumed
locate all scuff marks and clean with Mr. Clean eraser
move furniture, clean under and behind all furniture.
windows
baseboards
dust all surfaces, bookcases, tables
dust ceilings, corners of rooms, fans
microwave
oven
disinfect countertops (This is done several times a day at my house.)
barbecue grill
outdoor patio/deck
garage/tool area/seasonal items/yard tools
power wash garage, cement driveway, areas outside the house, stairs
hose off screens

spring clean your purse, tote bags, backpacks, briefcase
car/vac/steam carpets (Hire the job out or rent a machine and do it yourself. Consider only using hot water extraction. Guard against rubbing the surface of the carpet so that the fibers are not damaged.)

Together forever.

How to make cleaning fun

Start with a speciality coffee or tea

I always make sure I am ready for the day. It seems like I get more accomplished if I am not in my jammies and my hair and make up are done. Not sure why, this is but it works for me:

LOUD music

Invite a friend

OPEN windows when feasible

FUN food on cleaning days

DIFFUSE energizing oils or burn your favorite candle

The Purge

Before you begin on the deep purge, consider whether you have daily housekeeping habits. If you do, the purge may not be that complicated.

If you know that your daily and weekly habits need improvement, work on them first using the ideas listed earlier in this section. Work on the purging ideas on Fridays or when you have a couple hours of free time. Once you have worked through your home, you will find that maintenance will become so much easier. The goal is a clean and orderly home.

One of the most important concepts to living in an orderly home is to consider the space that is available to you and how you use that space. If it is too crowded, consider what you are using the space for currently. Reclaim your living space. Live in the space you own. My season of life involves a daughter moving to college, another daughter moving to a new home with her husband while a son is heading off to Air Force boot camp. As each change occurs, I aim to clean through the abandoned spaces thoughtfully. Two summers ago, I cleaned through two bedrooms, moved furniture, bought new bedding, painted walls, donated and refreshed our home. Instead of unused space full of stuff, these areas are cleaned out with just what we want to use.

The truth is that many of us have too much stuff. This is an ongoing challenge. Consider the time you spend on cleaning. Just imagine how it would feel to just restart how you interact in your home. I don't want to be a storage hoarder. At any stage of life this is easy to do. The ultimate goal is to have empty space, not tightly organized space. Often the challenge is to realize how much stuff we have so we are inspired to lighten our load. When you are organizing, put all of one category into one area. Gather all items related to that category from around the house. When all things from one group are in one place, you can determine when you have too much. Decide what will be donated and what will be kept.

The truth is when it comes to tidying or straightening many people stay crippled from the fear of being overwhelmed with the project. Some may say that they don't clean because they are too busy or too lazy. However, I believe most are stalled with fear. Fear comes from not feeling adequate to do it well and not understanding the order of cleaning. Some are gifted in sorting and cleaning while for others it takes more courage.

Trash, Donate, Organize

To declutter you must first throw away, donate, and then put away.

Imagine you are moving to a new home. You are forced to go through all parts of your home. All closets and cabinets have to be emptied. Decisions on what to keep and what will be useful in the future living space force donations and repurposing. When you do your seasonal cleaning or, if necessary, a purge, consider that you want to live in the space that you own. Envision that you are moving. Keep only what you would keep if you were moving. This visual helps me to be more ruthless in what I keep.

To be successful, one must make tidying an event. Do not try to combine it into the daily and weekly maintenance of a home. This means that this effort must be viewed as a project like remodeling a room or building on a deck. Fasten your seatbelt. The daily cleaning is more like putting things away. The seasonal cleaning is necessary to make the regular tidying feasible. When it comes to seasonal cleaning, anyone can do it. You just have to start with a plan and set your mind to it. You don't need to compare yourself to anyone else. Just yourself. You only have to be the best you, not someone else.

Don't think of trying to put things away until you have thrown things away. The first step is to begin. Select a small project that can be completed easily. Perhaps a drawer in the kitchen would be an easy place to start. Once the task is completed, build on that success. Feel energetic and confident as you tackle more sizable projects.

Zero in on your problem areas. Look for places where clutter accumulates. Begin by taking a notebook around your home, assess each room/space, and take some notes.

Identify the room. Note what you see in each room. Be honest. Be thorough.

Here is an example of what you might write:

Living Room Assessment
book bags by the door
rug full of leaves
clutter on the couch
shoes by the stairs
pillows on floor
laundry on the couch

Continue by listing clutter in each area of your home including your garage and vehicles.

Identify any large areas where you have piles of clutter. Once you have a written overview of the clutter and messes in your home, study it.

What can I learn?
What patterns emerge?
What might be contributing to my clutter?

large bulky items left out after grocery shopping
unfinished projects
coats not hung up
school bags or purses left on floor
items that need to be put in a cabinet or closet

cleaning products left out instead of underneath sinks or in laundry room

piles at the bottom of the stairs ready to go up or down

trash

empty packaging

clothes that need to be washed or put away

wires in messes near outlets or floor or visible near a desk

Once you identify the "what" and "where" of your clutter, pause. Imagine what you want your house to look like once you have purged all unnecessary items. Envision and write down what you would like to experience in your new clean and orderly home. Maybe you would like more space for people or a favorite activity. Perhaps you would like to enjoy a bath in an uncluttered bathroom. Consider that you would have a relaxing bedroom space with an efficient closet. Would you like to have guests over for meals? Identify your goals. Write out your intentions. Spell out your dreams. Visualize the new and improved space. Post them on your bathroom mirror. When the work is overwhelming, take a deep breath and imagine the end result.

My middle child has recently transformed her living spaces from an overwhelming amount of stuff to a space with just what she needs now. It's no surprise that her largest category was clothes followed by books earning a close second. As she entered the halfway point in college, she asked for help. I am very proud for all the hard decisions that she made as she threw things away, donated and then re-organized. Her space is so relaxing and inviting.

Purging is not something that is accomplished in a short period of time. It is a sort of resetting. It is much like moving. There is such a feeling of things being new. Drastic results require lots of work. When possible, set aside a group of days, or a day or half a day to complete a portion of the purging. Keep at it as time allows until you have exhausted all that needs to be purged. The finish line will bring you much joy!

⌐→

Getting Ready To Purge - What To Gather
Before you begin, gather these items:

> step ladder
>
> tape measure
>
> black garbage bags (Black bags will keep you from seeing items once you have decided to throw them away. Once discarded, don't reopen the bag to reevaluate.)
>
> Sharpies (black)
>
> 4x6 cards
>
> 2 medium sized boxes, plastic bins or large shopping bags (for donations)
>
> Note: To simplify the sorting, use the cards to write "trash," "donate," and "keep." Place these cards in front of boxes or baskets designated to hold these groups. Sharpies are handy when marking boxes or organizing containers.

⌐→

Prepare the back of your vehicle for donations. Clean out your trunk or back seat.

Setting your house in order is so rewarding. Great satisfaction occurs when you access the items you own and develop an awareness of the things that have fulfilled their life with you. When you find a new home for them through donation or throwing away, the sensation is so freeing. Imagine relaxing or enjoying in the space you own.

Key rules when seasonal cleaning or purging

1. Gather all items that are alike to one space. Plan to store all like items in the same location. While this seems simple, it is often challenging. As you begin on a category that needs cleaning, you may find that these items are scattered in numerous storage areas. Give this some thought and locate all like things together.

2. Do not buy organizing or storage containers until you are finished with the "Sort, Trash, Donate" plan. If you think about it, you really don't know what you need until you are finished cleaning out.

3. Expect to make a big mess while you are touching everything and making decisions. It is supposed to get worse before it gets better.

4. Take EVERYTHING out of your closet or cabinet when cleaning. Clean the inside of the closet. Wipe out. Vacuum out. Consider painting or putting liner down when necessary. A quick straightening up does not require taking everything out, but purging or seasonal cleaning highly suggests this method to keep only what you really need. Look for items that have lived their best life with you. Send them on their way. Feel free! Take all trash immediately to the outside garbage area or dumpster. All donations should be loaded into your car or piled so they can be dropped immediately. A helping friend comes in handy. They are not emotionally tied to your belongings and can gently help you decide to let go.

5. Once all trash and donate items are out of the house, sort out the things you plan to keep. Put all like items together in the same area. Use baskets or organizers that you have to reorganize the newly cleaned zone. Most cleaning situations do not require a trip to the store to buy new organizing tools. Only do that when necessary. Sometimes baskets that were used for storing things that you have not tossed or donated can now be repurposed for your newly organized space.

6. When organizing larger storage areas like attics or garages, consider buying containers that are the same size and are easily stacked. For example, my Christmas decorations used to be sorted into groups, but they were in a variety of boxes. I bought about thirty boxes that are grey and black and stackable for storage areas. Label each box. This is so helpful and extremely essential! I remember when I was changing the children's clothes out seasonally. Same-sized boxes which were properly labeled greatly aided that effort. This organizing tip really helped especially since I would not be getting back into them right away.

    By examining the usefulness or purpose or importance of the things you own, you are free to live happier in your space. You control your stuff. It does not control you.

Categories To Purge

Consider purging in the order of these categories.

The first category that you start with is CLOTHING;

Gather all your clothes from around your home into one large room. Empty your closets and drawers so all the clothing is in view.

Don't forget any clothing that is stored in extra closets. For most people this is overwhelming, but just trust me that this will bring you much contentment or mental peace.

Sort into these groups to speed up your efficiency:

socks, hosiery
undergarments
shoes
bags (purses, totes, evening bags, suitcases, garment bags)
accessories (scarves, belts, hats)
jewelry
tops (shirts, sweaters, jackets, cardigans)
bottoms (pants, skirts, shorts)
jackets, suits, coats, outerwear

Take a deep breath.

Establish three areas for sorting. Trash. Keep. Donate.

Many items fail to be useful or to bring us happy memories. Some items are kept because we do not want to be wasteful. This would be one of my problems. Some items are kept out of obligation. Perhaps your mother or a special friend gave you a piece of clothing that you feel obligated to keep. Ask if you love this selection and whether you want it to be part of your future wardrobe. Some items have finished their lives with you, so it is time for them to live in a new home.

Start by going through each category and applying the above divisions. For example, once all of the shoes are sorted in the above groups, put all shoes destined for "trash" in a black bag. Grab up all "donate" items and put them in the back of your vehicle. All items marked "keep," "hang," and "fold."

Here are questions to ask yourself when facing each item of clothing:

Does it fit?
Is it good quality?
Is it in condition?
Is it one of my favorites?
When did you wear this last?

Once all items have been sorted into trash, donate and keep, move any seasonal items into boxes that should be kept out of sight until needed. Don't forget to label the box! While some items are definitely fit for the extremes of each season, most clothing can be multi seasonal. Knowing this, don't spend a great deal of time taking the seasonal items out of your closet and resetting it twice a year. If space allows just grab the items that are not in season and set them toward the back of your closet. Pull forward season appropriate items. If you dress in layers, most clothing should be multi-purpose. I find that in the summer it is freezing inside buildings dictating that I keep a coat or sweater handy. In the colder season, the opposite is true asking me to shed my layers indoors.

An entire chapter could be written about knowing your style and selecting items that concur with that selection. If you are unsure of your style, consider your lifestyle and fit clothes accordingly. I aim to be classy and comfortable. While I need a variety of clothing for the diverse situations of my life, these overarching standards always apply. Specify and then simplify.

As a rule, you will have more storage space if you will fold your items. When you handle all of your clothing, you may notice a fray or stain or tear that you previously missed. Touching each piece of clothing that you will save allows you to remember what you own. Fold each item separately. Line up items in the drawers so the edge is facing up. Think of how you see clothing in a retail setting. By facing the edges up, you can see everything in the drawer at one glance.

For many people, opening the closet doors feels stressful. This could be because the closet is too small or because there are simply too many items inside. Regardless of the cause, folding as much as possible will free up more closet space. When hanging items, face the hanger where it curves to the left. All clothes should be facing the same direction. Hangers are placed facing into the closet allowing the owner to easily flip through them with their right hand. Outerwear should be hung on a hook or in a closet closest to the entryway.

Once you have purged your clothes, you are ready for the next step.

Second category is BOOKS;

As before, all books should be gathered into one area. Believe it or not, I have done this by force recently when my school room flooded. Fortunately, my bookcases were sitting up off the floor about eight inches, so none of my books were damaged. However, when resolving the situation, I sorted literally hundreds of books into the listed categories.

Questions to ask when sorting books:

Have I read this book? If so, it is likely that I will not read it again. This might be a time to donate. You have already gained the intended knowledge from the book. It is time to share it with someone else.

Unread books? Most books are read when they are acquired. If they are waiting for a time when you might read them, it might be time to let them go to a new home.

People with large book collections are almost always learners.

If you have never worked through your books, it might be a sizable collection. Once you have worked through this process, you may repeat it a few times until only the most coveted books are left.

Third category is PAPERS;

The goal here is to throw away or shred as much as possible. Really. Think of the classes you have taken which are represented by a notebook of notes. Have you taken the notes back out to read them? Likely, the answer is no. The benefit or value occurred when you took in the information. Live free. Throw away all of your notes.

Keep all papers, mail and catalogs in one spot. Go through everything and toss and shred as much as possible. In an office setting, sort papers into "respond," "file," and "shred."

Save the warranty, but not the manual, which can be found online.

Cards. I save cards for a few weeks. Then I select my favorites and toss the rest. Christmas cards with photos or stunning art are saved on a ring so that we can pray for them over and over throughout the year. The value of the card was completed when it was received and read.

Home Office Ideas

Set up your desk or office area based on your needs. Do you need to be in an area where you can see the children? Do you need quiet? Do you like windows? I do. I love to look outside as I work. For others the distraction of the outdoors is too much. If this is you, select a space away from windows. Do you like bright space? Are there enough electrical outlets where you want to work? Can you add an electrical strip? Do you need to be in a room dedicated to office work? Does your living space allow for a separate space?

Identify what type of storage you need. Do you need a wall organizer? Is there a closet in the room or selected area? Does it house only items that are used daily, weekly and monthly? Do items in the space need to be moved farther away to allow for more frequently used items? Identify an area in the desk or on top or under the desk for supplies such as paper, pencils, clips, legal pads, notepads, envelopes, stamps, and address labels. If needed, use a table or shelf for the printer and related ink and paper refills. Evaluate the light and change the light bulbs. Add or subtract lighting. Keep supplies like tape, stapler and hole punch together. Do what works best for your space and needs.

OTHER CATEGORIES to purge;
Other categories are much smaller and varied from household to household. Some relate to hobbies or crafts. Identify other categories for your home and tackle them in the same way as those listed previously. Some other groupings might be:

tools
kitchen items
small appliances
office items
workout equipment
electrical
musical
medicine
toys
collections

knickknacks

linens

floral

bathroom items such as makeup and toiletry supplies

different craft categories

sewing

photos

> I leave this category for the last of the list. As an avid scrapbooker, I hesitate to try to explain what to do with photos. Please do not leave them in magnetic albums. Mark them with post it notes so that the history associated with the photo will not be lost. Set aside time to sort them into large categories. Then sort those further. Consider scrapbooking in real paper? albums or digital albums or at least scanning them all into the computer for safe keeping. Perhaps the favorite ones could be made into large scale photos for sharing.

> Note: This should be considered a project and treated accordingly.

Create a photo wall for your family. These are well loved. Just today my sixteen year old hesitated on the stairs looking long at the newly hung photos of our family. This warms my heart. These are his people. Emphasize your people by hanging them on the walls in your home.

My baby.

One Christmas I ordered, for my mom, vinyl letters with my maiden family name and a quote that read, "Grandchildren complete the circle of love." Then I placed handsome black frames for her fourteen grandchildren on the wall. We replace those photos as the children grow. No doubt, most visitors are invited to view the "brag wall" in the hallway. What a simple way to experience happy endorphins!

One of my next plans is to create a wall full of the best loved photos from the decades of her life. My parents lived over fifty years together as missionaries. They celebrated marriage, family, four children and currently fourteen grandchildren and a myriad of adventures. What a thrill to be able to look at this wall full of memories. My daddy went to heaven about a year ago. A file is growing on my desktop as I compile some of the best photos of their lives. One day soon I will print them and start telling their story on a new wall. Check back with me. It is a dream that I am working on.

Laundry

Why complicate a simple task?

Laundry seems to be a burden to so many. Several moms have asked how our family does laundry. Perhaps the size of our family leads to the belief that we have a "system." All I can relate to them is how laundry works into our schedule. Once a system is in place, prepare to be flexible. Sometimes company adds extra loads with towels and sheets. Certain weeks include washing pillows and comforters. Seasons of life add sports laundry. For me a pattern, weekly schedule, quick response to the dryer buzzer, and designated laundry person contribute to a completed task. Here are some thoughts from our system that might inspire ideas for yours.

Tuesday is our first stay-at-home day of the week. So early Tuesday morning after making coffee, I begin the laundry for the week. I usually start the load of mixed colors. Dark clothes follow. Whites and delicates are last. Each time the dryer stops I try to respond immediately and fold all the items in the dryer. Piling the clothes in a mammoth stack to be folded at the end of the day creates extra stress and discouragement. Folding warm clothes keeps them from wrinkling. I have a soft basket on top of the dryer that holds all clean socks.

Along the wall each child has a clean clothes basket. The clothes coming out of the dryer are folded immediately and placed into the correct basket. We do have a laundry chute the comes down from the children's bathroom. One of the children is asked to change out the towels in the kids bathroom and throw the dirty ones down the laundry chute. Each child puts new sheets on their own bed and throws their sheets down the laundry chute. Purchasing two sets of sheets for each bed simplifies laundry and assists the process of making a bed quick when company is coming.

SORTING, FOLDING AND PUTTING AWAY PROMPTLY

By sorting the clothes as soon as they finish drying, they never escape the laundry room unfolded. This habit has kept a stack of clean items begging to be folded from ever appearing in any other part of my house. It seems to work best to face a stack of laundry coming out of the dryer, rather than requiring the committed time for folding when several loads are done. Less wrinkling happens when articles are folded promptly from a warm dryer. Once laundry is complete for the week, each child is asked to promptly take their clean clothes up to their room to put them away.

My sister tells me that she did things a little differently. "It was an all day affair to do laundry for the whole family. My husband usually took on this job. So I did our sheets and all towels and our clothes. When the kids were little, the two older girls worked together and the other two did their laundry together. I figured with Carissa and Adriana in charge it would be done. Within about a year, they all started doing their own laundry and have been for many years. It simplified our job tremendously and taught each of the children that skill early on."

HANGING AND SOAKING

Other essentials for success in my laundry room include the hanging bar for pieces needing a hanger immediately. Sweaters, delicates, sports clothes, men's dress shirts and no-dryer items rest on this fold-out bar until they are transferred to the correct closet.

Whenever possible, soak troublesome items between loads. A utility sink is such a blessing. When I cleaned houses in college, I would just drool when I had a utility sink to work with instead of a bathtub or outside hose. When we built our current home, I managed to locate one inside and one outside. They are such a help. My inside sink often holds a bucket of Biz dissolved into warm water. After soaking many notoriously stubborn stains disappear easily.

WHO IS IN CHARGE?

Each household must sort out who is in charge of the laundry. Dads often take over these jobs. In our home, the kids help me accomplish this activity. Each older teen takes a year to be in charge of the laundry so they will be confident in this task in college and later in their own home. Like most other housework, systems must be developed for your family and for the configuration of your home. Try ideas that fit your family's needs. Always think of ways to bring the process to more efficiency. I love when a new idea saves me time or solves a problem.

BRIGHT AND ORGANIZED

Bright colored walls in my laundry room with friendly signs brighten the chore. A rug in front of my machines is a must as I slipped several times due to the moisture in the room. Whenever baskets and clever organizing items simplify the task, the process seems more enjoyable.

THANKFUL FOR MY DRYER

A cross-stitched sign that I made as a new bride hangs in my laundry room. It reads, "I am thankful for my dryer." I am truly thankful. As a young girl living in the West Indies and even the Carolinas, I hung wet clothes out to dry. We dashed out to gather them up if a surprise rain storm appeared. While my appreciation for today's dryer is acute, I do miss the smell of clothes that have been dried in the sun. They remind me of many happy memories of childhood.

Create a time in your weekly schedule to attack your laundry. Respond quickly to each buzzer. Set the timer, if neccessary(I have to). Share the responsibility with family members. Think of how easy things are when they work with a rhythm. Devise a flow that func-tions for you! Don't complicate a simple task!

Car Organizing

Think about the time you spend in your car. If you have children, you might be transporting them to and from school daily. Perhaps you are taking them to sports practice and games along with a myriad of other things. Or do you drive by yourself most of the time? Whatever your situation, your vehicle is almost an extension of your home. Below are a few ideas:

Used bags under the driver's seat. When you are approaching home or filling up your gas tank, pass a bag around the car asking for people's garbage. If by yourself, always empty trash from your car while you are waiting for your gas or parking in the garage. While the vehicle is in motion and kiddos are strapped in their seats, you might receive cooperation and a quick response. Train them early on this habit if you can. Most of us park very near the outside garbage cans. This maintains a trash free zone.

If your vehicle allows, pack healthy snacks in case you are delayed unexpectedly. If you are heading out for an extended time, you can pack perishable items in a cooler such as cheese sticks, boiled eggs and cut veggies. For non-perishable snacks, consider crackers, granola bars, pretzels and beef jerky.

While the children in your vehicle might be just perfect, mine were always fighting over who would sit where. No appeal to fairness or kindness motivated independent resolution. So, my response was to assign seats. Sometime I rotated them on the first of the month or on the three transitional times mentioned earlier in chapter one: January, June and August. For my family, we added these essentials to our vehicle:

windex wipes
clorox wipes
baby wipes
(You need them even if you don't have babies.)

kleenexes

hand sanitizer

audio books (Our favorite was anything Odyssey. Truth is that one family road trip with 64 hours of drive time ahead, I loaded over 80 hours of odyssey prior to leaving. This kept everyone quiet and occupied as we drove.)

small broom/dust pan

coupon pouch

large pocket file for receipts

note paper/pens/pencils

Items to keep little ones busy

2-3 shopping bags to keep numerous loose items from running around

bag of returns (when necessary) This keeps them out of the house and allows me to complete the return quicker when we are passing near the store.

Blessing Bags

A blessing bag is a Ziplock bag of need items for the homeless we might encounter. Items in this bag might be a toothbrush, toothpaste, hand cleaner, snacks such as beef jerky and crackers, water bottle, apple sauce, warm socks, gum, granola bar, comb, deodorant, Chick-Fil-A gift card, card with info about local mission or Salvation Army shelter. Do you remember the extra travel size toiletries that you brought home from your last trip? This bag and the hospitality idea in the hospitality chapter would be a great use for those items.

Assign a child to clean out all vehicles as part of your one day a week family cleaning spree. If you are on your own, drive through a car wash as needed or put it on your weekly or monthly schedule if you want to do it at home.

One idea that worked for me when my kids were little was to pull up to one of those outdoor vacuums. Encourage every rider to clean up their space. Pick up the trunk and the floor. Vacuum and recruit helpers as your reach is challenged. In my group of five children, I had two that really loved to vacuum out cars. Strangely, my recently sent boot camper did not like to do weekly contributions and frequently volunteered to vacuum and clean out all the vehicles as his contribution. He did a great job at it too.

Where not to store items:

⌒⌒

Parent's Homes

Speaking of parents homes often become the dumping ground for boxes, odd items, memorabilia, clothing, baby items, etc. If your stuff is at your mom's home, free her and go get it. Make decisions. Let her live her best life with the space that belongs to her. Don't let mom store things that do not belong to her. If you are the mom, empower yourself. Consider what items are being stored in your home that are not yours. Send pictures to the owners. Ask what they want to do with them. Establish deadlines. Clear out these items so you can live freely in the space you own. For many, storing their kids' things is taking over entire bedrooms or portions of the home. Be brave and purge.

On a final note, let me mention something that applies to my season of life. For all practical purposes, four of my five children have moved out. While I am new to this experience, I know that my house seems to be growing, unlike the sensation of shrinking as the kids grew. We are talking about downsizing, but the kids protest as they want to come back to this house. For now, we are staying put. So, I am working on deep cleaning and repurposing the spaces they leave behind.

One of my children cleaned up her room and packed up before she left for college. Sadly, the others left lacking this skill of maturity. The aftermath resulted in the deep cleaning of the deserted closets, drawers, under bed space, hanging clothes and miscellaneous. I cannot fathom wanting others to decide what is important to me, what to keep and what to throw out. However, as I work toward completing this book, another room awaits my attention. My fourth child just left for Air Force boot camp with a stack up to my knees of dirty clothes piled in his closet. If you knew me well, you would not suspect me of exaggeration.

Laundry finally completed, his younger brother and I sorted clothes into keep for later for Josh, donate to the boys' home or just throw away. Some items are being stored with his name in the attic. Yes, I wish that he had made these decisions. He was asked to work through these areas before he left. The reality is that it will be done soon so that this space is ready for its new life. Bunk beds are being sold. Carpets will be cleaned. All spaces cleaned out thoroughly. I just repaired walls and painted the room last year, so it will soon be ready for a new queen bed and fresh bedding.

Last night my mother created a conference call and asked several of us about some of my dad's belongings. My dad went to heaven about a year ago. While we already completed an intense clean out of his office and closet, many decisions loom. Work hard to keep your home from becoming a storage area for your children's items. Also, don't consider your mom's home a place for storage either. As you might imagine, this is a common problem. Many parents of grown children are burdened with full storage areas, crowded garages and unchanged guest rooms. For all practical purposes, they are not living in their spaces. Their homes are storage. Break free. Clean out the garage. Clean out the attic. Clean out the unoccupied children's bedrooms. Clean out the outside storage shed. Clean out the overflowing closets. Reclaim space for today's life.

My mother is moving across town to be closer to my brothers and their young families. Moving forces cleaning out. She is working through envisioning her new space as a location where she can live in every area. Think of it as a new season. Don't be sad to make changes. Focus on the outcome. Gear up for the thought that cleaning out is work. Many decisions must be made. A sizable mess will likely be created before the work is done. In the end, great satisfaction in a fresh, livable space promises to overwhelm you with satisfaction and joy.

Imagine the newly cleaned space transformed into new living space. Dream it. Make it happen.

Storage Units

Additional storage units are big business these days. While you might suspect that they are used for transition, more often they are rented to store overflow. If this idea applies to you, it is time to purge and conquer this burden. Freedom is in your future. You can do it.

Conclusion

You can't enjoy the simple pleasures of life if you are always running around at warp speed trying to keep up. Aim to create a home that promotes peace, respite and easy hospitality. I like for my home to communicate relaxation so it will renew those who live it in as well as those who visit. Identify how you intend to live in your space. Consider how your space makes you feel now. How do you want to feel when you come into your space? I want my kids to love coming home. I want my husband to look forward to coming in the door from work. I want my friends to thrill to come over for a cup of coffee and a long chat. I want my house to smell clean and delicious. I want my home to invite time curled up with a blanket. I want the routines and rhythms in my home to create a consistent invitation for welcoming. I want life and energy to be reflected in my home. I want the comfort of the furnishings to invite long conversations and rest when we are tired. I want the messages in the verses to inspire and change minds and actions. I want the history in the photographs to convey memories of trips, of people loved and a life well lived. Concisely, I want the rhythms and routines of our home to allow us to live our best life hum in our home and listen to the hum our home.

US.

Three

FOOD

"She looks well to the ways of her household..."

PROVERBS 31:26 ESV

*A*ll of us need to eat. Keeping a home well requires that food be fetched, organized, planned, prepared and cleaned up after. All this takes practice, skill and strategy. If you were like me, you might have spent a great deal of time beside your mother or grandmother in the kitchen when you were growing up.

My parents were church planters, so that meant we were weekly responsible for food related events. It might be the Sunday morning spread, a ladies event, a week of camp kitchen, men's breakfast or preparing for visitors for Sunday lunch in our home. Food was a consistent need. As an adult, I have organized and run the kitchens behind church camps, three day events feeding 700+ people, weddings, funeral receptions, conferences, and more. It is clear that I do love working with food and the hospitality that surrounds it. Perhaps your experience was different. Maybe you were never involved in the activities required to put food on the table. It may be that your mom never asked you to help or that your family always ate out or ate prepared food requiring the microwave. Since one of the biggest sources of daily stress in the home is what food to prepare for each meal, tackle the questions of what you need to buy, what you need to eat, how to serve or pack food efficiently and how to clean up easily.

Whatever your background or current situation, a home full of homemade goodness is possible.

For purposes of organization, let's start at the beginning.

Pantry and Refrigerator

What non-perishables do you need in your pantry? A well-stocked pantry is like money in the bank. So, check the list below. While the list could be much greater and should be adjusted based on your family's likes and dietary restrictions, these items seem to be a must.

Start by taking all expired items out of the refrigerator. Never be intimidated by your refrigerator. Think of it as a closet. At your grocery store the newest dated items are rotated to the back to ensure that the oldest items are used first. Always, always check dates for expired food. Store your meat and cheeses in the drawers to secure the coldest storage. Consider adding a liner to spaces where fruit and veggies are being stored to absorb moisture and limit spoilage. When your habits include washing all fruit and veggies along with cutting them as you plan to use them, less will spoil.

Remove all items from the shelves.
Plan for zones or groupings.

canned items
jars
snacks
cereal/oatmeal
pasta
produce that does not need to be refrigerated like onions and potatoes
drinks (tea, sodas, coffee)
plastics (plastic storage bags, garbage bags, cling wrap, foil)
Store as much in your pantry as possible. Stock up on staples.

Basics
bread
yeast
olive oil
coconut oil
salt
pepper
apple cider vinegar
white vinegar

Baking items
chocolate chips
Nutella
flour - all purpose, wheat (keep in refrigerator as it is not prepared with chemicals to withstand bugs)
baking soda and baking powder
cocoa powder (unsweetened)
evaporated milk
condensed milk

pure vanilla extract
lemon extract

Sweeteners
raw sugar
Truvia
granulated sugar
confectioners' sugar
brown sugar
maple syrup
honey

Drinks
coffee
tea bags
hot chocolate
cider

Grains, Rice and Pasta
wheat berries (if you make wheat flour or homemade bread)
dry peas and beans
rice (white and brown)
quinoa
couscous
noodles (based on your family's needs)
breadcrumbs (plain or panko)

Cereal and Snacks
crackers (Saltines, Wheat Thins, Triscuits, Ritz)
chips
pita chips

tortillas

cookies

dried fruit (raisins, apricots, or cherries)

peanut butter

almond butter

applesauce

breakfast cereal

rolled oats

almonds and other nuts

Canned Goods

chicken broth

beef broth (some need to be stored in the refrigerator)

black beans

white beans

red beans

baked beans

green beans

peas

white corn

yellow corn

creamed corn

salsa

canned tomatoes

tomato paste

Herbs and Spices

garlic salt

cayenne pepper

chili powder

crushed red pepper

curry powder
granulated garlic
ground cinnamon
ground cloves
ground cumin
ground ginger
oregano, basil, parsley
Italian seasoning
paprika
sesame seeds
poppy seeds
thyme
nutmeg

Refrigerator
Dairy
milk (organic or 1%)
creamer
greek yogurt
vanilla yogurt
salted butter
colby cheese
cheddar cheese
parmesan cheese
mozzarella cheese
goat cheese
feta cheese
eggs

Fresh Fruit and Vegetables
avocados
carrots

celery
tomatoes (Fresh from garden in the summer. Off season we buy on
the vine and cherry tomatoes.)
broccoli
cauliflower
brussel sprouts
bell peppers
greens (baby kale, spinach)
mixed greens
romaine lettuce
potatoes (sweet, white, or new)
onions
garlic
lemons
tomatoes
bananas
onions
potatoes
apples
bananas

Condiments
peanut butter
ketchup
mustard
mayonnaise (Miracle Whip at our house)
salad dressings (our favorites are poppy seed and vinaigrettes)
hummus
salsa
jelly
jam

local jam and jelly
barbecue sauces

Freezer
boneless chicken breast
ground chicken
ground turkey
ground beef
slab bacon
turkey sausage
frozen vegetables from the summer
(favorites are blanched tomatoes, corn and okra)
frozen spinach
frozen berries (blueberries, mixed berries, strawberries, cherries, mangos)
pecans (when I can get them)
pie crust (my favorite is the Pillsbury pie crust to make quiche)
Blue Bell ice cream (Is there such a thing as your favorite flavor? They
are all just sinfully delicious.)
Add items that fit your family's likings.

Staple Shopping List
produce
bakery
meat & seafood
dairy
frozen
canned goods
baking
snacks
condiments
baby

pet care
cleaning/household
paper/plastic
toiletries beauty/personal care

Stockpile - Supply Stash

This list can be used to buy non-perishable essentials in bulk to keep the weekly bill down. They include grocery, freezer and toiletry items. Bulk shopping saves money, trips to the grocery store and most importantly, it saves time. Before going on this outing, survey your pantry, freezer and bathrooms for current supplies and upcoming needs. If you work this plan, you will find that sometimes you are well stocked on an essential which adjusts your purchasing quantity for the next run. Then sometimes you find you need to increase your quantity because you underestimated your needs. The details of this list vary each shopping trip as we have quite a bit of family and company.

BAKING SUPPLIES
chocolate chips
nutella
flour
yeast
salt
granulated sugar
powdered sugar
brown sugar
baking powder

baking soda
corn meal
flour
salt
granulated sugar
powdered sugar
corn starch
cocoa
vanilla extract
cooking oil (canola, olive, etc.)
spices
honey (buy local when possible)
brown sugar
raw sugar
sweetened condensed milk
nuts
white vinegar
apple cider vinegar

Add your family's items to personalize this list.

FROZEN
frozen vegetables
frozen fruit
frozen fish
ice cream

BREAKFAST
cereal
oatmeal

syrup
pancake mix
muffin mix

LUNCH AND DINNER
canned meats (tuna, samon, chicken, etc.)
broth (chicken, beef, etc.)
rice
pasta
beans
peanut butter
jelly or jam
tomato-based products (sauce, paste, stewed, crushed, etc.)
canned fruits and vegetables
soup
dried fruits and vegetables

SNACKS
chips
popcorn
pretzels/chips
ice cream

CONDIMENTS
ketchup
mustard
mayonnaise
salad dressing
barbecue sauce

DRINKS
water bottles (for coolers)
coffee
tea
soda
juice

TOILETRIES
Just a top: I shop for many of the first items on this list at T.J. Maxx and others at Walgreens. Go where you find the best price.
soap (hand soap, shower gel)
shampoo
conditioner
hair products (gel, mouse, hair spray)
lotion
deodorant (his and hers)
toothbrushes
toothpaste
mouthwash
razors
shaving cream or shaving soap
aftershave
feminine products

HEALTHCARE
bandages
bug spray
sunscreen for body and face
lip balm
moisturizer

over the counter (OTC) meds (aspirin, ibuprofen, cough drops, mela-
tonin, etc.)
vitamin C
prescription meds

CLEANING SUPPLIES
glass cleaner
laundry detergent
dish liquid
dishwasher detergent
dish sponges
Swiffer liquid/pads
white vinegar

PAPER AND PLASTIC GOODS
toilet paper (difficult to estimate - buy this on sale)
paper towels
napkins
trash bags
freezer bags (quart and gallon)
sandwich bags
foil
plastic wrap
wax paper

HOUSEHOLD GOODS
batteries
light bulbs
candles (Can you have too many of these?)
matches

OTHER
baby supplies (formula, diapers, wipes,
etc.) pet supplies (food, litter, etc.)
bandaids
other first aid products

Bulk Cooking

Bulk cooking is a not-so-secret idea that is relatively easy to implement. Once operating with this system, you'll discover there is less anxiety over food preparation in your home. The basic idea is that you prepare food in bulk to minimize your clean up and save time. Let me explain a few scenarios where bulk cooking minimizes spending and food preparation time.

Young Couple

Katie & Zach.

Take Katie and Zach, who are a newly married couple. On Saturday they go to the farmer's market which is in walking distance of their new little apartment. This market is well stocked with local produce, as well as with meat from a nearby farm. With this fresh meat and produce selected for the week, Katie sits down on Saturday evenings to plan meals from their finds at the market. With the advantages of a grocery pick-up system, she orders the ingredients she needs from her grocery store. Sunday mornings this young couple attends church. On the way home they swing by the grocery store and pull up to the designated area where their groceries are delivered and loaded into their car.

Once home for the afternoon, one of them prepares lunch while the other prepares food for the week ahead. My impression is that Zach usually makes lunch while Katie starts the bulk cooking for the week ahead. Since Zach consistently takes his lunch with him, she cooks all the meat and sides so that he will have healthy lunches just ready to heat up. She eats her meals at school or while working from home. When doing bento boxes, all ten boxes are prepared at once.

A favorite breakfast is a slice of quiche with a smoothie. So, Katie bags frozen fruit in separate bags to allow for a grab and go process in the mornings. The quiche is cooked so that a slice can be cut and heated quickly in the early mornings. An evening meal of poppy seed chicken is prepared ahead of time and covered with foil eliminating food prep for the day-of. Without going into more details, you can imagine how helpful this process is to save time and money. Eating this way controls food costs of eating out frequently as well as ensuring that this couple will be eating healthier options. This happens to be a true story of my newly married daughter and her husband. By helping me as a young girl, she learned this system and implemented it immediately.

Family

Imagine a young family with five growing children. Mom and Dad are both overwhelmed with responsibilities of parenting and keeping a home while meeting all the needs of their family. Let's call this mom, Jan. In an effort to save money, Jan shops the sales she sees on food for the week. She watches the cycles for sales on her family's favorite meat and vegetables. Using the ideas mentioned above in this chapter, she bulk shops as she spots frequently used items at their lowest price in the sale cycle. To determine the best time to buy some of her family's favorite items, she asks workers at the store about the best time of the week and month to shop for her favorites.

Prior to going to pick up food, she quickly assesses and cleans her pantry and refrigerator. Now she knows what she needs to incorporate into her menus and identifies the needs. In an effort to bring down her weekly grocery bill and spend less time shopping and food prep-ping, she located some extra cash to bulk shop non-perishable essen-tials for a three month period. Actually, she is really proud of this. She sold a few unused items that were being stored in the garage to (give her this extra cash (this is where you sing, "woohoo, woohoo," and do the happy dance). As an extra happy, her hubby has been bragging on her for taking such care of their family!

Jan decides to grocery shop on Fridays and bulk cook on Saturday mornings. She washes and slices all of the produce. Breakfast options are prepped. Portable lunches that her husband and children need for the week are prepared. Meat dishes are prepared along with salad items and vegetables for evening meals. Snacks are bagged and shelved in the pan-try on the snack shelf and in the snack drawer in the refrigerator. Done.

Think of the time that Jan saved. Everyday the food is predeter-mined. Much of the preparation and clean-up is already done because she has completed so much in advance.

Jan continues to see the benefits of bulk shopping and bulk cooking for her family. As she grows in her abilities to work these ideas, she pro-cesses food for two weeks at a time. The greater her efforts, the more time and money she saves. As a side benefit, she finds it easy to invite others to join them for a meal. Sometimes she prepares an extra main dish. This comes in handy when someone needs a meal quickly. Emergency situations with sickness, deaths and other challenges occur more often that we can imagine. With practice, this routine of homemaking allows Jan to be more compassionate and hospitable. She reaches out with a meal to be the hands of Christ. Although she took meals from time to time before implementing this system, she knows that she is more eager to offer generosity now. This is a win-win in so many respects.

Once Jan locates the best deals on meat and produce, and accesses the current items at home, she develops a meal plan. Then she locates all she needs for meals at home, packed meals and snacks. No more daily stress about what to eat for snacks, supper or where to pick up food. There is a confident calm because she has a plan. If you think about it, Jan is like the Proverbs 31 woman in verses 14b-15a (ESV) when she brings in her food from a distance: "She gets up before dawn to prepare breakfast for her household . . ." Yes, that is her." High five!

I think we can apply verses 26-29 here too: "When she speaks, her words are wise, and she gives instructions with kindness. She carefully watches everything in her household and suffers nothing from laziness. Her children stand and bless her. Her husband praises her: There are many virtuous and capable women in the world, but you surpass them all!"

If you feed people, they feel cared for. This is truth.

Couple or Single
Consider yet another scenario. My girl does not have children, so it might seem that she does not need to bulk cook or bulk shop.

However, she is still busy with her job or volunteering or caregiving or taking care of her grown children. For the sake of an example, she could be an empty nester, a single gal or maybe a retiree. The age does not matter. The concept is that she is preparing food for just herself and maybe one other. Let's call her "Lily" (I love that name).

The process of bulk shopping and bulk cooking is much the same. Access what needs to be purchased for non-perishables for the pantry, freezer and toiletry items. Shop these for a one, two, or three-month period. As this effort is repeated, a more accurate list will emerge. Remember to stay flexible.

For bulk cooking, determine the meats and veggies that are on sale and seasonably available. Create a 1-week or 2-week menu based on breakfast, lunch and dinner needs. Select a day for shopping or pick up. Select a day or part of a day for food preparation. Enjoy saving money and time. Enjoy knowing what's for breakfast, lunch and dinner.

Lily experiences a greater freedom to be generous. With the bulk shopping and bulk cooking, she might double or quadruple a meal allowing her to slip extra meals into the freezer. When I was a newly married woman, I took meals for all sorts of reasons. Food is a great way to give a hug. I took meals to those in our church community, to people at my husband's work and to neighbors. Lily, or anyone practicing some of these ideas, can plan to put up extra for the numerous opportunities allowing her to practice being the hands of Christ.

Just imagine how easy it would be for Lily to entertain company in her home. Hospitality could be expected or sudden. Life is like this. Sometimes we can plan it, but often it is sudden. Many meals are easy to stretch when you are well stocked. Some meals are crazy easy to expand and share.

As I write, my largest stock pot filled with a ham bone and water is preparing for one of my husband's favorite meals. He loves split pea soup. It will be perfect by the time he arrives home from work. If I needed to share this meal, I could easily double what I am making and add more sides. I am stocked and ready.

HOW TO BULK COOK

If this book included lists of recipes and specific instructions for bulk cooking, it would have to be customized to each household. Cookbooks and books on bulk cooking already exist in the market. If you are a confident cook, just start researching this idea. If you are new, start with simple meals. If you are just beginning all of your experience with food preparation and kitchen management, explore recipe books and blogs that teach cooking. Ask someone in your life who is fantastic with food to share their most well received and well loved meals. Most people who are excellent at something are thrilled to be asked to teach someone what they know well.

This section will demonstrate how to plan what works best for your situation.

1. Look through what you have in your pantry and freezer. Incorporate what you already have purchased. This only costs you time. Using what you already have saves you from making the purchase again. It also keeps you from wasting food that has to be thrown out when it expires. You do not purchase items that you already have because you know your inventory. You may need to look back to what items make up a well stocked pantry and add some of these to your supplies.

2. Determine the length of time you will need to prepare food for as you bulk cook. Let's start with one week.

3. Write down "breakfast," "lunch," and "dinner." Allow for space to write food plans for seven days under each of these. Plan all the breakfast meals first, then lunches, then suppers (see example below). If you are keen on saving money, look through the weekly sale flyers where you will be picking up food. An alternate start to this process might be to start by writ-ing down dinner plans for the weeks to come. Later, once you are in a routine with dinner, add breakfast and lunch plans.

4. Based on your current supplies, make a list of what you need. Sort your food needs into categories of like items. I sort by areas of the grocery store. For example, if you follow my list in the previous section, it will take you to the right side of the grocery store, through the middle, across the back and then up the left side. I really aim to stay in order and not back track. Laugh at this, I know. Almost every sizable trip to the store has me on a hunt for one or more items they have moved. Consider ordering your food online where this service is op-tional. It saves so much time. Also, you can send a teenager or your husband to pick it up. That is happening right now as I write. My college daughter is picking up our groceries. I smile because this is wonderful. I ordered them last night online.

5. Pick up your groceries. Unload. Keep in mind if you are work-ing a system like this, you will not be buying very much that is not on your list because you know what you have. You built a stockpile for items you use all the time. Your list should be shorter. Your weekly cost should shrink. Honestly, the only time this does not work for us is when I send my husband to the store. He is a very enthusiastic person who loves to go to the grocery store. He buys what is on the list, but adds lots of other "fun" food. Maybe you have one of these at your house too. If you are this person, I don't know how to help other than to have you

identify your goals which will help you stick to the list. One of the most exciting changes to grocery shopping has been the online shopping with the pick up outside the store the next day. I love this option. When shopping for many new items or just buying a sizable number of things, the pick-up is quite a time saver. By being thoughtful in food planning, trips to the grocery store should be limited. Going frequently to pick up "just a few things" adds great cost to your budget.

6. Keep all produce out on the counter. Wash and cut all fruit and veggies for the week. Bag and store. Exceptions might be bananas and apples stored on the counter for grab and go snacks.

7. Cook for the week ahead. I usually start with the meat or the main dishes for the evening since they are more time consuming. Store all food in containers or bags they will be used in. Store in proper portions. If you are making lunches for the week, distribute them into containers or bags that make grab and go easier for the morning rush. Check out bento boxes for lunch. They fun up the process. I am a snob and only like YETI cooler packs for lunch boxes and coolers. The cooler packs stay cold so long and do not leak. What else could you ask for?

8. Stand back and look at your refrigerator shelves. Admire all the stacked containers and bagged food. Congratulate yourself for all of your hard work. Contemplate knowing all week what food is available. Anticipate the fast grab for the rush hour in the morning for work and school. Enjoy not being anxious as the dinner hour approaches. Your food is prepped or mostly ready to cook or just heat.

A helpful hint for your prep time would be to keep the prep day meal simple. It might even be pizza or something in your Instapot. Consider using paper products to ensure a quick and easy clean up.

A few notes on bulk cooking:

If you live the homeschool lifestyle like our family or pack up everyone for school and work, this system of preparing in bulk works beautifully. Breakfast is ready to go with minimal mess. You pull up to the 11am protein snack break ready to eat cut veggies and hummus. Maybe your kids like protein smoothies like mine at break. Because you are preparing food ahead, your valuable homeschool time can remain just that. As you finish schooling for the day, there is no stress about what to make for dinner. Decisions are already made. No energy is expended on what to make. Just pull your meal out to cook without investing time in food preparation. Minimal prep and minimal clean up.

Taking a meal is greatly simplified when you plan ahead. Create a duplicate of a meal that you are cooking for your family. Add a dessert and salad and a meal is ready to share. Prepare this meal in disposable tins so no dishes will need to be washed or returned.

Just a quick note on caregivers. Please develop a sensitivity to this group of people. They are all around us. Look for parents of handicapped children, adult children caring for aging parents, family caring for their loved ones suffering with cancer or ALS or a myriad of diseases. Often the weak or sick person is given treatment and attention is paid to their needs. However, the caregiver usually implements the transportation, movement, and nursing–often to their own neglect. Be sensitive to these people. Look for them. Take them a meal or muffins or frozen main dishes. See a need and meet it.

Example of one week of meal planning:

Custom build your own week or two of meal planning. Once your meals are determined you can list the items you need once you evaluate your inventory. You may ask what might be on a list of meals at our house. Here is a sampling:

Breakfast
    avocado toast/fried egg/fruit
    oatmeal with toppings
    scrambled eggs/turkey/toast/fruit
    avocado toast/fried egg/fruit
    oatmeal with toppings
    scrambled eggs/turkey/toast/fruit
    oatmeal

Lunch
    salad in a jar
    broccoli soup/garlic toast/veggie tray
    chicken fingers/veggie tray
    chicken noodle soup/veggie tray
    salad in a jar
    tortilla soup/veggie tray
    sandwiches/fruit/veggies

Dinner
    baked chicken/potatoes/peas
    salmon/broccoli/couscous
    chicken strips/potato/asparagus/salad
    tilapia/rice/peas/salad
    split pea soup/cornbread
    shredded chicken/grated cheese/chips (one of the guys' favorites)
        with fruit and cheese
    poppy seed chicken/salad

Bulk Cooking To Create Freezer Meals

The concept of bulk cooking is one that speaks to prudence, being prepared ahead and efficiency. During my young life I cooked for a camp kitchen. I have cooked for over 750 people who ate from our kitchen over a three day period. I have prepared food for weddings, for funerals, for class parties, for large Christmas parties, for POW Christmas lunches and even a boys' home. People always need to eat, several times a day. Food is a universal language. When people are fed, they feel loved. This is not a Bible verse, but it is a truth.

Truth is found in Proverbs 22:9 (NLT), "Blessed are those who are generous, because they feed the poor." Sometimes I am feeding people who are physically poor. Other times, I am feeding people to nourish their souls.

All of the above situations have required cooking ahead and freezing prepared food so that we could serve hungry people well. My most important job has been wifing for thirty years and parenting for twenty six years. As I write these numbers, I should have you know that I am not as old as these numbers indicate. Denial is a real thing.

In doing this most important job of homemaking, my family has strongly identified some favorite foods. Someone suggested I attempt the daunting task of writing a cookbook. This is not that, but I will include some of my favorite recipes. I am more of a simple cook. I cook with the freshest ingredients that I can locate to create dishes. I am a master of reformatting leftovers. This comes from necessity in my young years, followed by a strong sense of not wanting to waste food or money.

A cardinal rule for stocking your freezer with prepared meals and prepped food is to label and date all items. Always label and date everything going into your freezer. Finding a mystery bag is just not fun.

When considering bulk cooking to fill your freezer with meals ahead, motivate yourself with scenarios like this one. Imagine yourself during the week busy with your job, homeschooling, or other responsibilities.

Wouldn't it be wonderful to know that your freezer was full of possibilities of meals already prepared? Consider the ease of pulling out a chicken dish and cooking it with steamed vegetables and a tray of warm, homemade chocolate chip cookies. Envision a day full of unexpected happenings which delays your arrival home. No worries. Select a prepared dinner from the freezer. No need to pick up expensive, processed food on the way home. Imagine finding out suddenly that a friend's husband is coming home from the hospital this afternoon. Because you have meals put up, it is easy to pull out a lasagna and begin cooking it. Add a quick tossed salad and garlic bread and you have a warm meal that meets the need you see. Magic? No. The benefit of routines and rhythms that allow you to be generous? Yes!

A bulk cooking event at my house goes something like this:

Decide what is going to be cooked based on the needs of the event or family schedule.

Clean out the freezer.

Itemize what you do have in the freezer.

Choose recipes for food you will cook (start simple.)

Identify a shopping list.

Plan the containers for storing in the freezer. I love glass containers 9"x13", 8"x8" and freezer Ziploc bags of all sizes. Be well stocked on these items.

Whenever possible, store in Ziploc bags because you'll use your freezer space more efficiently when you can seal the bags and lay them flat on top of each other. Be sure to use freezer bags not storage bags.

Shop the list. Select the day you will cook. Buy all dry ingredients at least one day ahead. Please don't try doing both the shopping and the cooking on the same day! It's too much!

My bulk cooking does include quite a bit of meat, so I often run out very early on the cooking date to pick up the meat. Although I have two refrigerators, I usually cannot hold all of the meat and refrigerated ingredients at once.

Clear the kitchen counters except for needed ingredients.

Create prepping stations and cooking areas based on space and helpers.

Begin early on your cooking day.

Drink something yummy while you cook.

Consider playing loud music.

Know that your kitchen will be messy.

Engage your children to help. They will need to know these skills.

While I am not frivolous about what I count for a school day, I would count this for a school day. Imagine if they taught this skill at school. You have some lucky kids who can work alongside you. Be sure to give an inspirational talk along these lines before starting to cooking.

Wear a Williams Sonoma apron. If you can, have everyone who is helping wear an apron. It keeps your clothes clean, adds to the fun factor, makes all helpers look official.

Plan to be happy.

Plan to have pizza or very simple food for supper.

Clean up everything before you finish for the day.

Take a long, well-deserved bath at the end of your work.

Smile!!! You are awesome!!

An alternative to bulk cooking all in one day might be to double or quadruple the main dish recipes that you cook regularly. This works well for a situation where a half or whole day cannot be located. Develop the habit of tucking leftovers in the freezer after you have eaten them once or before you leave for vacation. On days when you most need them, you will smile because you have a stash which makes you look and feel like super mom. I see you smiling. If you are not already doing this, try it.

Bulk cooking for freezing is great to do at the beginning of a season like right after the Christmas holidays or as the summer begins or right before the fall schedule kicks into gear. I always bulk cooked heavily right before I had a new baby. Since I don't live close to my extended family, I have imagined how great it would be if my family came over to bulk cook together on a regular basis. Someday, I might create a club with three other friends where we help each other bulk cook or trade dishes.

The greatest advantages of living this way are saving money and time. The time investment is greatly returned in time saved. Cooking and cleaning up the kitchen in one long setting certainly saves hours of time when compared to cooking each meal individually. Curiosity might also lead you to ask how much savings occur from bulk cooking for your freezer. From conversations with two of my other cook friends, these meals average about $1 per serving. If you organize a lunch meal for a function that is brought in, you can reasonably expect the cost to be $10-$15. For evening meals or fancy functions, the price per person goes up from there. It is not unusual to expect to pay $25-$30 per person for a meal at a venue. So, your meals cost less and your ingredients are higher quality.

Doing bulk cooking for my freezer is work, but Galatians 6:9 (NLT) advises me, "So let's not get tired of doing what is good. At just the right time we will reap a harvest of blessing if we don't give up."

While I bulk cook for my freezer primarily for ease in running my home, the recipes I selected had to meet certain criteria. When I first started this process in my early marriage days, I resolved not to do any cooking with canned soups because of the dangerously high sodium. I also focused on foods that have a greater quantity of meat that are not high in carbs. My family does not prefer casseroles. Select foods that meet your family's dietary needs and pleases their taste buds. Once you have done a few cooking ahead for freezer days, the process will speed up.

Remember some recipes are cooked and then frozen, while others are frozen and then cooked.

Recipes for some of these dishes are listed in the back of this book in the appendix.

FAVORITE FOODS TO FREEZE
Main Dishes:

chicken cordon bleu
stuffed beef tenderloin
chicken marsala
poppy seed chicken
turkey lasagna
spinach lasagna
veggie lasagna
peabody lasagna
gotcha lasagna
meat loaf
shepherd's pie
shrimp stir fry
beef stir fry
chicken stir fry
fried rice with shrimp
fried rice with chicken
calzones
frozen peppers

double stuffed potatoes
taco stuffed pasta shells
meatballs
meatballs with spinach
sausage manicotti
turkey enchiladas

Breakfast Meals:

breakfast burritos
spinach & cheese quiche

Other:

cooked bacon (you will have to hide this)
cooked ground meat
cooked shredded chicken
cooked shredded roast (add bbq sauce to any of the shredded
    meat to create some kind of yum)
ground turkey with taco seasoning
chocolate chip cookie dough
bags of frozen fruit for smoothies
cut sausage sautéed
ham pieces (ready for quiche)
sausage pieces (ready for quiche)
biscuits (cut and frozen before they rise)
frozen veggies from the farmer's market when in season
(i blanch and freeze at least three boxes of garden tomatoes each
    season for sauces)

HOW I SHOP FOR FOOD FOR MY FAMILY? WHERE DO I SHOP?

Since this is an anticipated question, I will preface my answer by saying that I am great at overthinking. I am not proud of this quality. In an effort to find the very best for my family and be prudent with the funds that God has given us, I tend to fetch food from several locations.

Mennonite Store - 2-3 times a year

We pick up 25 lb-50 lb bags of dry goods from the Mennonite store which is located about an hour away. These items are more pure than you can find in a traditional food store. They shelve 1-5 pound bags to sell to the general public. When requesting the larger portions, they are glad to sell to like-minded homemakers. The food we purchase is raw sugar, organic brown rice, oatmeal, wheat berries (for wheat flour and making bread), beans (split peas and seven bean mix). Storage for these items are in 5 gallon buckets with a gamma lid. Keeping dry goods in air tight containers eliminates access to bugs and moisture. While they don't last forever, they do last quite a long time. Just for fun we pick up pints of their special peanut butter honey to enjoy for a few weeks. Then we sit for one of their amazing fresh sandwiches. This run makes a pleasant day trip. Turn this into a date on a Saturday with your hubby or an outing with a friend. Or grab the kids, do school on the road and consider it a field trip. Just be sure to call ahead if you need one of the large bags of dry goods so it will be waiting on you.

Sam's Wholesale Club - Once a month

It is nearly impossible to go in and out of Sam's without spending $100 or more because nearly everything is more than $10. Bulk sizing is the name of the game there. My plan is to keep to the perimeter of the store. I practice a strong resolve especially since they have books in the middle of the store. How can you browse through books without settling on one or two that you really must buy? My runs to Sam's occur only once a month. The list of needs include salted butter, produce, 16 oz disposable coffee cups, spices, frozen fish (especially mahi mahi and tilapia), frozen berries (blueberry, mixed berries, strawberries, mango), couscous, and ground turkey. Substitute Costco if it is your choice of wholesale shopping locations.

Sprouts - Once a month
Because we have limited resources for fresh food in our area, I love the meat counter at Sprouts. This is a relatively new store for us. My favorite items are their slab bacon, organic boneless, skinless chicken breast (I buy 30 lbs at a time), and lean beef in pinwheels or beef tips.

Farmer's Market - April through August - Once a week
Based on availability, I buy all the fruit and vegetables that our family can eat that week. During these months, I rarely buy produce elsewhere unless it comes from another region of the country.

Kroger - Once a week
Pick up food with a sizable haul once a month. Smaller pickups occur on the other three weeks. This is really more of a fill in stop. I buy things here when I am out and need a quick pick up. Or I buy things that are just general grocery items that are not best bought in bulk. Obviously, I buy most perishable dairy items at Kroger. This store offers the shop ahead and pick up option which saves money and time.

Walgreens - Once every three weeks
Walgreens seems to run most items on sale in a three week cycle. The best deals at Walgreens during sales are in hair products, toothpaste,

toothbrushes, Emergen-C, paper towels, toilet paper and select snack products and gum in multiple packs.

Cooler Packing

Assembling salads in a jar.

Salads in a jar.

Learning to pack a great cooler comes in handy for road trips, several days of competition, sports practices that occur during dinner time, a picnic at the park and numerous other times. Coolers promise delicious foods that are really popular with our family. The truth is that we would rather eat out of our cooler than pick it up. Once again, this habit saves both time and money while offering a super yummy option.

What to pack in a cooler:

    salads in a jar (see recipe ideas in the appendix)
    sandwiches (special bread, quality meats)
    (our favorite sandwiches are croissants with lunch meat, muenster
        cheese and greens and chicken salad)
    cut fruit
    cut veggies
    cheese sticks
    hummus
    guacamole
    boiled eggs
    fried eggs (for breakfast sandwiches)
    pre-cooked bacon (do we need an excuse for bacon?)
    apple sauce
    yogurt
    chips
    cookies
    brownies
    favorite drinks
    water bottles

For hot meals at your destination, you may create a meal and freeze it ahead. Some situations will allow for a crockpot to heat up stew, soup or any appropriately selected foods. This idea works well when you are going on a vacation where you will be preparing your own meals.

Select a cooler that fits your needs. Consider whether you use the cooler in the car or outside. Does it need to fit behind a seat in the car or between seats in the van? Does it need to sit beside you at an outdoor event when your children are practicing sports or if you are tailgating? If your family is like ours, you might need more than one cooler. We have three.

If possible keep them inside to ensure they are clean and ready to go. If you must keep them in the garage, cover them to limit your cleaning time before you use them. Wipe the cooler when you finish using it and before you pack it. Chances are it needs both cleanings to be at its best. Leave your cooler open to dry after you empty and clean it if you want to avoid surprise odors and mildew later.

Use ice packs instead of water because it is cleaner and avoids leakage into your packed foods and outside the cooler.

Prepare your cooler food ahead of the day you need it. The day we travel, the cooler is already cleaned, open and waiting in front of the refrigerator to be loaded. If you are traveling to an event and packing foods that will be transferred to another refrigerator, freezing some of the foods might be best. Remember that your cooler is likely the last thing you load in the car.

When space allows, you might load one cooler with your drinks and another one with your food.

My youngest is a quick learner. When we need to travel, he jumps in to assemble sandwiches, cut fruit and veggies, compile salads in jars, gather plastic utensils and organize the drinks. We rely heavily on him because he packs suitcases and bags tightly in the vehicle.

Contemplate what items are heavier when packing your cooler. For example, we use a cooler most often for road travel and tournaments. Usually, I position the drinks and salads in a jar on the bottom or sides of the cooler which leaves the sandwiches and softer items on the top. Some items such as boiled eggs need to be as close as possible to the ice pack. I am very nervous about food poisoning, so eggs only go when I can be sure they are eaten early in the day. On particularly long days, the sandwich spread is a honey mustard or poppy seed dressing to avoid the risk of sickness with spoiled mayonnaise.

Non-food items that are helpful for every cooler are hand sanitizer, paper plates, napkins, plastic silverware, salt, pepper, mayo packets, paring knife, can opener, ziplock bags and some sort of clean up paraphernalia like Lysol wipes and paper towels.

Packing Lunches

Similar to the food list above, lunches for work and school consist of prepared ahead foods that are packaged for travel. Bento boxes are seriously so fun. With potential foods placed in an assembly line fashion and a few instructions, the kids can do the packing of lunches for the week ahead. For our family, packing lunches usually occurs on Sunday afternoons. While eating foods from home usually saves money over fast food or eating out, the real advantage lies in seriously loving your personally selected foods. If you are packing lunches from home, this process allows you to control the quality of your food and assists in eliminating the added salt and sugar in processed food.

When all five of my children were at home, we traveled extensively for speech and debate competitions throughout the school year. As cooler packing pros, the children stubbornly insisted on eating out of the cooler on road trip days as well as on competition days. The younger boys discovered that they could eat more without waiting when they were hungry, if the cooler was properly packed. Just to say, my kids are the biggest fans of ensuring that we have a cooler packed when we travel.

For intentional parents who commit to raising capable, independent kids who become competent, self-sufficient adults, it is vital to include them in this preparation process. In the years when we needed about 30 sandwiches or 15 salads in jars for the week ahead, the kids evaluated the work and knocked it out. Teamwork tastes good later. Somehow anticipating the results increased the enthusiasm to complete the job well.

The children who are living away from home are continuing the tradition by packing their coolers regularly. My married daughter received a cooler with their monogram on it for a wedding gift. How clever! Maybe the giver enjoyed a similar lifestyle to our family's experience. In just a year and a half of marriage, the newly married couple have just about worn out that cooler.

Snack Drawer in the Refrigerator and Pantry

To make life easier, select a space in your pantry and one in your refrigerator for grab and go snacks for the little and not-so-little people. If they know what is designated for them to snack on, it is less likely that meal ingredients will disappear. No guarantees here, but the concept works well most of the time. Recently, I was fixing a taco bar for about twenty-five extended family members. The queso cheese was quickly discovered by my 16 year old man-sized child who promptly located companion chips and devoured more than half of the family size container. Since we were not at home, the grab and go concept seemed to include all foods available. Seriously, my kids were and are frequently hungry outside meal times. Planning for snacks is essential.

Conclusion

If all of this is new, tackle one area at a time. Establishing routines and rhythms is all about doing family better. Saving time in the kitchen in preparation and clean up means more time together. It creates the hum you are desiring for your home. Saving money means more funds directed elsewhere. Homemaking is work. It takes lots of practice. Apply some of these ideas to generate an easier flow to the everyday in your home. Aim to sit around your table and give God thanks together each day. As you engage in conversation, share the best part of the day with each other. When possible, use your best things on the table. Learn to set a pretty table. Teach your children to set a proper table so they will practice family and hospitality too. Remember in the end that people are more important than things. Celebrate your people!

Four

HOSPITALITY

"Show hospitality to one another without grumbling."

I PETER 4:9 ESV

Generous living in your home enables you to love your family and others well.

My life has been a journey full of exchanges in hospitality. Growing up, my parents served as church planters in multiple locations. My friends and church community consisted of a rainbow of beautiful faces from my dark, Caribbean friends, to my Polynesian friends, to my Caucasian friends. Each culture brought its customs, it celebrations, its foods, its family life and its magnanimity. Numerous situations come to my mind as I contemplate the joys in being the receiver of generosity as well as the giver. Without a doubt the greater joy is being the giver. This chapter is about generosity and hospitality. Let me say that I am grateful to be married to a man who loves to be hospitable just as much as I do.

My life as a missionary kid started on the small island of St.Lucia in the southern end of the Caribbean. The homes were not much more than palm branches held together by mud. People often unloaded from a bus late in the afternoon at the end of our road as they returned from work. They would pause and bathe from a waist high tap of public water because there was no running water in their homes. Needless to say, extreme poverty was normal in this third world country. Yet, in our community of Christ-loving believers, generosity was never lacking. Since we lived on an island, fruit was in abundance. Most weeks when believers gathered to worship, they brought bags of collected fruit to share.

As my mother went into the villages to speak to the women, I, as the daughter of this very fair-faced lady, tagged along as a sidekick. Visiting showed honor. We would stop to visit or ask about their family. Always they offered food. Many times we left with a gift of fruit or an item they crafted like a tote bag from the palm leaves. A spirit of generosity shone amid this life of nominal material wealth.

The overwhelming generosity of local Polynesian friends in Hawaii cannot be properly expressed. My family was hospitable before we came to Hawaii, but we were greeted by gift giving, food sharing and the love of a new ohana ("family" in Hawaiian) Even all these years later, the friendships of our Hawaiian friends run deep. We communicate by phone and email. We do life together regularly even though we are separated by distance. It is impossible to out-give, out-love or out-feed any of these friends. Believe me, I have tried.

I remember with fondness being part of my family. We often lacked what we needed physically, but we had each other. Most days we ate around the table together. We were very loved.

Before becoming a missionary, my mother grew up as war orphan in a small town of Florida. As God tugged on her heart, she discovered her love for the Lord compelled her to offer her life to full time ministry for Christ. Once she completed her secondary education degree, and married my father, she entered her life's work on the mission field. She brought class and graciousness as she worked with the ladies that she discipled.

My mother's life has been an example of generosity and hospitality throughout all the years I have known her. She served her family well while balancing family, homeschooling, women's ministry, children's ministry and all areas supporting my father. She also typed and edited all of his graduate work. I am blessed that there was a hum in our home as my mother created rhythms and routines.

Her life lived out Col 3:2 (ESV), "Set your minds on things that are above, not on things that are on earth."

With more stories than I can possibly share, her sense of hospitality dominates my memory today. I ask myself, how did I experience this lifestyle as I was growing up? It began long before I was a thought.

My father always thought himself to be a poor, uneducated man. He ran away from home before he finished high school not able to read well. While he was working at a factory with his brother, two older neighbor ladies often fed this hungry looking young man. When invited to church by these same ladies, he agreed. You could say that the hospitality shown by these two retired ladies brought a young man to church. He found forgiveness in a Savior. His gratefulness led him to want to share this great news with others. This led him to read his Bible every free moment after work, apply for Bible school, train for the ministry, marry a pretty, Floridian girl that he met in college and spend the next 50 years in the ministry of loving on and discipling others for Christ. He used to say he was just a beggar helping other beggars find bread. He and my mom were really nothing spectacular, but they were available. Throughout their lives hospitality and generosity were often keys that opened relationships to the gospel. Humans gravitate to this message. The acts of charity from one human being to another often seem so other worldly because kindness and unselfishness are not inherent in most human interactions.

One of the frequent experiences that I have encountered in my daily relationship with Christ is how specifically he speaks to me through the regular reading of His Word. Today was no exception. One verse I read today is Proverbs 11: 25 (NLT): "The generous will prosper; those who refresh others will themselves be refreshed." In communicating about generosity and hospitality, few verses could be more appropriate. This scripture verifies my points here well. "A generous person will prosper…" Truth is that as you give, you are filled. The giver is receiving even more by the blessing of open-handed, abundant and bountiful deeds. Wow!

Even though my father eventually earned two master's degrees, he found it humbling that God would choose to use him to reach others for Christ. He gravitated to people that others might find too poor or too lowly. In kindness, he would loan our vehicle to others who needed it. He shared tools, trailers and his books. My parents frequently invited people to our home on Sundays spontaneously. On Sundays there was always enough in the crockpot to feed our family and one more family. We usually did not know who was coming. It might have been a family from the church or maybe a new family that was visiting. I have tried to carry on this tradition of having extra people for lunch or dinner. Our home is open to be used for hospitality on Sundays and other days as well.

My sister, Daphne, carries on this tradition of generosity by housing women from a local recovery ministry for months. Numerous people are greeted with food and laughter around their table. She is blessed to be married to a fellow who is also an excellent cook with a benevolent heart.

While I cannot be overly specific, my brother, Nathan, has risked his life to share Bibles in a closed country. This did not originate through an organized religious organization, but through a conversation during a business transaction. Time and again I have watched him give to those in need from his kind heart. Along with his wife, he offers kindness to others.

My baby brother, Titus, practices his kind and indulgent nature by adopting children. At the time of this writing, he and his wife have adopted three children who are not theirs biologically, but grew in their hearts before they were even born. The entire extended family and a community of friends are awaiting at least one more little person to join this family through the foster-to-adopt program.

Isn't he cute? We are on a golf date.

I married a generous man who, like me, loves to love on others. He too comes from a long line of givers. He is giving with his time and finances. Hospitality is a frequent action for both of us. Either one of us has permission to suddenly bring needy people home. It happens. One time I brought a mom, three boys and their dog and a great deal of stuff home. Suddenly. Tim just smiled.

This spirit of prolific, open-handedness overflows in my husband's family as well. His grandfather and father were famous for gifts of funds and time to an unknown crowd of people. Both of his parents gave quietly to provide Christian college education for students. They were captivated by many mission opportunities.

While they have both been gone for some time, my husband is still stopped by strangers who tell him about a before unknown kindness.

My husband's sister, Holly, and her husband, give in discreet ways to ministries through the benefits of their business. She is a clever baker and runs events with her skills to raise money for missions.

If you come from a long line of givers, then it should be easy to duplicate. If this is new, then begin a fresh pattern for generations behind you to follow.

⌣⟶

Receiving Kindness

Think of when you have been on the receiving end of kindness.

Long ago, we met a crippled vet and his wife. Like many others, we were invited for a meal in their home so often that we felt we could take our shoes off at the door as we entered. Important people and just regular folk would all pile into their place for a meal most weeks. Several times a week, but always on Sunday, their home was full. You might imagine that they lived in a fancy house or maybe a big place conducive to handling lots of people and lots of food. Not even close. Their home was old and worn. The carpets and furniture might even have warranted replacement. It did not look like a maid had been there recently. You could not conduct a white glove test.

Several tables were set out with mismatched chairs. Sometimes we ate from paper products. Sometimes inconsistent plates and cups filled the counters. Sometimes the variety reminded me of the contrasts of the people filling their home.

Mostly, we were thrilled to be invited into that noisy crowd of conversation. Everyone wanted to be invited. A quick look around indicated that maybe everyone had been invited. These were happy memories full of interesting talk and warm friendship. People from church came. People who would never be at church sat with us. This was generous hospitality.

More recently, I have noticed a trend. One of my daughters has been on the receiving end of a kind and generous young married woman in her mid-twenties who has purposely converted her spare room into a haven of hospitality. She frequently uses her room for people who need a place to stay for a few days or weeks. It is not primarily for her guests, but those who are in need of nurturing. She offers her key with a tag that reads "home."

When your home is open and ready for hospitality, the focus is on the people in the home, not the physical home. There is a saying that I gained when I married a Southern boy, "If you are coming to see the house, call ahead. If you are coming to see us, come on in." So the lesson applied communicates that we should stay prepared for guests, because living with open hearts means living with open doors.

Be hungry for conversation and willing to serve an easy meal if necessary. It is about the people. Be more about the quality conversation than impressing guests with your property or perfectly prepared food. Remember that the people that are fed feel cared for and loved. Isn't it about doing life and community? Don't worry about the unfinished to-do list. Don't feel sucked into creating a "Pinterest perfect" life before company arrives.

I am reminded that we need to be on the lookout for those who are vulnerable and wounded. Take them in. Offer healing. Rescue them from intense loneliness and isolation. It is a difficult and lengthy assignment. But it is worth it.

Folks don't mind if you invite them to jump in and help you set the table or toss a salad. Some of the best conversations happen when we invited people in spontaneously. Authenticity is welcomed and appreciated.

When inviting people into your home for coffee, a meal or overnight, communicate that you value their relationship. That is why you invited them. You don't care about making impressions. You care about them.

My siblings and I spent many years in Hawaii. Along the way we picked up a favorite family meal called "Hawaiian Haystack." In fact, three of us had this meal for our rehearsal dinner meal. The last deacon party in our home served this meal. It was a hit. Use this menu or the Mexican Party Bar for large group events where each attendee can bring a sizable portion of one ingredient.

⌒⌒

Ways to Practice Generosity

Looking for opportunities to be magnanimous is easy. Once you initiate your search, you will notice needs all around you.

Recently, my fourth child, Joshua, attended an extended family celebration with his father. One of the children along on that adventure was a special needs boy about eleven years old. All day, Josh engaged him by playing in the pool and involving him in other games. At the end of the day, the boy's mother, who had been watching closely all day, approached Josh to thank him for being so kind. The mother asked my husband how he raised such a boy. We really do not have an answer for that question other than to say that we encourage kindness. We encourage generosity. We encourage including others.

Josh with his cousins.

Gifts seem to an obvious response to needs. Sometimes this is just perfect. In an effort to be an awesome gift giver, listen. Listen and even take notes (I take secret notes on my phone so I won't forget the great gift ideas I think of while I get to know my family and friends better). Being a listener lets you meet needs better.

Meeting a need may mean taking a meal. If your home runs with some of the ideas in the food section, sharing food isn't complicated.

⌒

Preparation is Everything: Set Yourself Up for Success

Because being appreciated is critical to feeling loved, don't fail to gift those who invest time and energy into your life and the lives of your family. Write a thank you note promptly for a gift or kind gesture. For efficiency, create a note basket with return address labels, stamps and a current address list.

When invited to a party or for a meal or to stay in someone's home, be sure to bring a hospitality gift. It is strange that this even needs to be stated, but it does. Prepare by having a shelf space or drawer where you keep gifts, gift bags and tags for impromptu gifting as well as planned appreciation.

Teachers, coaches and neighbors treasure being thanked. Some simple ideas include consumables such as special hand soaps, kitchen towels (from Williams Sonoma), blankets, and themed baskets. Since we are from Tennessee, everyone assumes we all eat barbecue every day (which is almost right). We do eat Chick-fil-A almost every day. However, if your home area is clearly popular for something, you might consider themed gifts as hospitality gifts when you travel. A gift bag with several locally concocted barbecue sauces combined with something else kitchen friendly is always met with excitement.

⌒

Secrets of Preparing for Christmas Well

Christmas is easily the busiest time of the year. Over the years that I have been responsible for Christmas as an adult, I have practiced a pattern that generates efficiency and calmness in my heart as I aim to execute Christmas well. I wanted to share this because so often the thought of doing Christmas well creates panic and a desire to disappear. Christmas can be overwhelming. If I waited until Thanksgiving to do anything for Christmas, I would definitely run away! For women who are single, married, mothers with children, empty nesting, or grandmothers, there is really so much to do during the holiday season.

Here is what I found works for me:

1. At the beginning of October decide that it is time to begin preparing for Christmas.
2. Begin making lists in your planner. Make decisions.
3. Make a list of teachers, coaches and neighbors that you will gift.
4. Create a budget.
5. Brainstorm about gifts that you will buy. Thinking about this with the budget planned first is key.
6. List your family members and start brainstorming for the gifts that you will buy.
7. Update your Christmas card address list.
8. If possible, take your family Christmas picture or select your favorite one from this year.
9. Order your Christmas cards. Address your envelopes when they arrive. This is a process. I aim to mail these cards the day

after Thanksgiving. It is not stressful at that time, because it is done. The same amount of work needs to be done, I just have fun doing it ahead of time. Doing it in a rush is just stressful and no fun.

10. If possible, check your bag and paper stash. Buy extra tissue paper, tags and scotch tape. One Christmas as my Josh was going to wrap Christmas gifts that he had bought for his siblings, I discovered that we were out of tape. I promised to buy some the next day. He was entirely too impatient. In no time, he had them wrapped in Christmas wrap with duct tape.

11. Look at the calendar so you can recruit helpers. I select the second or third weekend of November to decorate. I pull all the Christmas decorations down from the attic near the end of the week. I sort all the boxes. Boxes for tree go near the tree. All others go in the foyer. The tree is put up and lit. Normally, my favorite kitty remembers what is magical about laying under the Christmas tree lights on the tree skirt! I love this. I am smiling as I type. This is his new normal all season. I used to work with a decorator decorating homes for Christmas. We started in mid-October. Most homes were fully decorated in one or maybe two days inside and out. As I decorate my own home, I have a rule. Set aside one day for decorating. Do all that can be done. Then, put everything away. I put up the tree a few days ahead so I can be sure the tree stays lit. I complete everything but the tree. Then I focus on the tree, put up all boxes and vacuum. Whatever did not get put up in that one day will have to be used next year. This plan is freeing. The season is just about to begin, but I am ready. No stress. Just calm.

12. In October once I have a budget and specific plan for Christmas gifts, I begin by buying for the teachers, coaches, neighbors, close friends and co-workers. When all the kids

were living at home, there were many years that the teacher-and-coach count for five kids averaged between seventy and eighty. So, I aimed to show our appreciation with $2 gifts. Some of my repeated gifts were the hot chocolate packets with biscotti, an iron mail holder ($15 marked down to $1 at Hallmark) and bags of homemade goodies. When these items are secured, it is best to wrap or bag and tag them. Store in baskets ready to go. Sadly, these baskets usually end up in my room. My room becomes the prep-for-Christmas space. With so many kiddos, I never had a wrapping station other than the floor in my bedroom. Raise your hand if this is the location for your wrapping station.

13. Think about what to buy for neighbors. Usually, we baked. I always prioritize neighbor relationships.

14. Listen carefully when you are with those who are on your Christmas list. Buy thoughtfully. Stay in budget as much as you can.

15. Christmas stockings are fun to shop for throughout those months. I was sad thinking that the kids might be outgrowing that fun. When I tried to mention that I was sad about this, loud protests broke out. I guess that they do not want to stop the stocking tradition. So, I told them that the stockings would be given out to anyone that is at home on Christmas morning. I did not want to think through mailing or transporting stockings. About a week before Christmas, I actually stuff the stockings. I started this because when I did it the night before, some stockings were overloaded while others were just lacking. Starting a few days early helps me ensure that they are just perfect.

16. Since our goal is kindness toward others, our family has found great pleasure in either crafting or just purposeful

gifting to those we encounter during the Christmas season or even other times of the year. Since I worked as a waitress, cleaned houses and worked some retail early in my life, I have true compassion for those in service jobs. The holidays are especially challenging as more people are out shopping. People are hurried, grouchy and often unkind. My idea is to give an ornament or food item with a purposefully written tag which reads something like, "Wishing you a very merry CHRISTmas," "We appreciate your kindness," or "Giving you a little something just to ensure that you have a blessed CHRISTmas." Sometimes I write our verse on the back. One year I made the tags with our picture on one side and a verse and appreciation on the other. The response from those at a drive through window, a register or at a restaurant is delightful. Everyone appreciates being valued and appreciated. What an easy way to spread Christmas cheer and be the hands of Christ in kindness. Once again, the key to this idea is to collect these items and bag and tag them early. Set them aside and be ready.

My big idea about Christmas is this: it is about giving, not receiving. The season is only a few weeks long. Enjoy all the music and gathering that you can possibly imagine! To do this well, I aim to complete the work of Christmas early. This allows me to limit stress and maximize the important things: focusing on reading the advent to my kids every day, going to as many musical functions as possible, hosting a Christmas party for friends at my husband's request, finding situations to meet needs together as family, drinking hot chocolate and watching Hallmark movies, going to beautifully decorated Christmas places and just people watching, caroling for friends, and as a gift, in places where people are lonely or sick, singing with family and friends around the piano or with my guitar, going with family to deliver our gifts to neighbors or just be at home together enjoying each other's company.

Not everyone thinks it is fun starting so early preparing for Christmas, but I dislike last minute stress. If I am busy getting ready for Christmas in December, I will miss it completely. Even if my body is attending functions and activities, my mind will be busy working. Remember in Proverbs 22: 3 (ESV) that, "A prudent person foresees danger and takes precautions."

So, my motivation for working ahead is to ward off stress. These ideas allow me to be present at Christmas. Since we are talking about creating the hum of the home, I know that I have to work ahead, or I will not be humming.

Ideas for Generosity

COOKIE CLUB

Cookies are one of the best things ever. Everyone loves cookies. This club is simple to implement in several settings. An example might be how this club is implemented in an adult life group. Say the group is about 50 members strong. Visitors come frequently. The group wants to be friendly as well as invite people to come again. So, ladies that want to sign up take a plate of cookies to visitors. When a visitor comes, one of the class members who lives nearby and is part of the cookies club follows these ideas.

1. Cookies must be homemade. (No bags of Oreos please.)
2. Bake 1-2 dozen of your favorite cookies.

3. Place cookies on a sturdy paper plate or fun container.
4. Write a friendly note stating that you are glad they came to visit. Sign your name, phone number and any other information you want to share. For example, if you have something in common, here is a great place to mention similarities.
5. Deliver in person by Friday of the week they visit.

The big idea is that you want them to come back. You want them to feel loved. You invite them into your community. Your delicious act of kindness and hospitality is a hug telling them that they are important to you and the class they just visited. Lastly, it is just fun. It is guaranteed to make new friends. Wouldn't you want to be friends with someone that brought homemade cookies to your door?

⌐⟶

POW (Prisoners of War) Christmas Luncheon
One of the best things we can teach our children is the joy of giving. The past two Decembers several of our children served Christmas dinner to some of our local World War II veterans. The children listened to their inspiring stories and gifted them with thank you notes. What a privilege that our children could be exposed to these men who bravely served our country. My children served with a group of their homeschool friends.

Event planning starts in the late summer as students from around our area read biographical sketches about each soldier. These brave young men courageously approached war, survived capture and captivity and returned home with not so great memories. Several told of their Christmas in a prisoner of war camp. One told of being turned in to the enemy for the equivalent of a United States dollar. All humbly accepted the attention and gifts from students and local businesses. This experience is a win-win for all involved. The students read more about WWII. Often veterans' stories prompted reading or discussion as new questions are brought up about geography or history. Our students wrote notes to each soldier. Students spent extra time during the week compiling the boxes and preparing goodies for the tables. Recently an anonymous donor sponsored the event at the famous Peabody Venetian Room. The organizer of the event gathered help from friends. My group of homeschool friends collected magnolia leaves, pine branches and nandina berries for the decorations. The students distributed drinks and desserts. They visited with each Veteran giving them the gift of listening to their stories.

What a gift to meet these unsung heroes.

Warrior Center - Drug and Alcohol Recovery Men's Center

Another event which has become an annual tradition for our family has been Christmas at the Warrior Center. Our life group class meets at midnight in our church parking lot, then we travel as a convoy to the warrior center, which is an alcohol and drug treatment center.

Our friend, a Messianic Jewish, goes door to door waking up residents, instructing them to come to the kitchen for an early morning breakfast and gifts. Our children help with the cooking and serve the residents. It's a very touching experience

Families adopt a resident or two to gift with a warm pair of work gloves and a winter hat. Each receive a Bible to encourage them in their growth.

BLESSING BAGS

The blessing bags mentioned under car organization are a great way to show spontaneous generosity.

Christmas time offers numerous ways to share and give to others. Our family also loves to make Samaritan's Purse Christmas boxes.

This year, directly after we delivered presents to the Warrior Center, a special thing happened. My son, who was spending Christmas in San Antonio, Texas, at the Air Force Boot Camp, experienced a touch of kindness on Christmas Eve as he attended a service on base. As they entered the service, several people from the local church brought gifts of brownies and cookies for the soldiers. We gave to those here in our hometown while others gave to our son.

Small gestures mean a great deal.

⟜⟶

Helping Your Family to be Successful

While this seems to go without saying, I will say it. Being aware of ways we can help our own family be successful is important. Whether it is finding ways to bring a child alongside his sibling to connect one in helping the other, or if it means spending a week with your mom helping her clean out after your dad goes to heaven. Whatever it takes, I believe that we should do life with our immediate and extended family. If you open your heart and mind, God will show you so many ways to help our family to thrive.

⟜⟶

Hospitality Habits

One of the greatest gifts we share with others is kindness. As mentioned before, hospitality has played a significant role in all the relationships in my life. When I was a little girl, we hurried around on Saturday and Sunday preparing food for Sunday lunch. Although we did not know who would come, we anticipated that we would invite a first time visitor to church or someone who needed some extra love. Nowadays, around our table on Sunday as well as other days, we welcome our growing kids along with their friends. These shared meals offer more than satisfied hunger. Conversation builds friendships. Camaraderie solidifies trust. Commonness reinforces strength.

Hospitality expands past the togetherness surrounding a meal to the minuscule efforts extended by a generous heart in planned and unplanned moments. Think about ways in which you can offer hospitality. If you plan ahead just slightly, the joy of offering a warm reception to a neighbor, welcome to an unexpected opportunity to visit, or generosity to someone who suddenly needs a place to stay, promises bubble up into a place of delight in your life. So, here are some ideas for establishing habits of hospitality.

1. START IMMEDIATELY.

Make up your mind to prepare to be neighborly and open your home intentionally to family, friends and strangers. Begin by searching for times to invite someone in when your house is not perfect and you don't anticipate a visit. Savor the idea of generosity toward others. Recall times where you have been met by a warm welcome. Be that for those God places in your path.

Once a friend found herself unexpectedly without a home. They were forced to move out suddenly overnight on an icy, cold night. As morning came they were nearly frozen from the sleet and rain they had endured over the night hours of moving furniture and possessions.

This situation only reached my attention in the early morning. Unprepared, but willing, I invited them to stay in our home. What could I offer? My kindness. Clean beds. Warm food. Hot showers. Needed rest. Safe haven. Friendship. This story is not about me. It is about opportunity.

Once a neighbor called me, anxious about fifteen international children that needed a place to stay for the weekend on short notice. Between us she figured we could house and feed them. She was right. We housed and fed those kiddos for four days. Even years later, memories of this weekend bring a smile to my face. One of my daughters remains so impacted by this encounter that she wants to adopt internationally.

Ask God for eyes to see the needs already all around you.

2. LOOK FOR OPPORTUNITIES.

Don't outsource hospitality. Instead of family and friends going out to eat, invite them to your home. Keep the food simple so the focus is on togetherness. Gathering in a home usually extends the time and blessing of conversation. Ask everyone to bring something to create an easy meal. Cooking in bulk frees you to invite guests without warning as well as share food with those facing unexpected tragedies.

Think about relationships that need to be deepened. Bond with groups that you do life with on a weekly basis. The invitations don't have to always include a full meal. Gather for snacks or just dessert. It is more about being together than what you eat. Consider what you can offer and plan accordingly.

3. KEEP FOOD FOR SURPRISES.

A simple bag of gourmet cookies put back (or in hiding as in the freezer marked 'liver') or a pitcher of lemonade whipped up quickly both offer a welcome when an unexpected guest stops by.

Bake or cook in bulk so extra food can be thawed quickly when needed. Since I was privileged to grow up with many Japanese friends, we mastered the habits of gift giving. In Hawaii, our Japanese friends often stopped by for a short chat. Since they regularly arrived with a gift in hand, we practiced being prepared by baking sweet breads and putting them in the freezer. With these gifts ready for unexpected guests, we consistently presented our friends with tangible appreciation for their friendship.

Gift giving for me today includes my homemade bread, homemade jams, local honey, scripture gifts, a book, hydrangeas from my backyard, chocolate chip cookies, or just whatever we can share from our kitchen.

4. FOCUS ON YOUR GUESTS, NOT YOUR IMPERFECT HOUSE.

When you anticipate company, start with clean linens on the bed and a stack of fresh towels. Lay out a few extra blankets and if possible a soft and a firm pillow. Organize a few extra toiletry items into a basket in their room or the bathroom. Add a water bottle and a welcome note which includes the wifi number and perhaps a house key on a friendly ring.

While we do aim to keep our home clean and picked up, it stays in the "lived-in" look on most days. My goal is to welcome you, not wow you. So, I invite my guests to "come on."

5. SHARING INSTEAD OF IMPRESSING.

The focus when offering hospitality should be about sharing your home, your time, and mostly yourself. Carefully consider the conversation. Are you meeting the needs of your guests? Is the talk about you or them? Is the tone uplifting or depressing? Is your conversation encouraging?

While honoring my guests by picking up and checking to be sure the nearest bathroom is clean, I don't obsess about impressing. This frees me to enjoy my friend and bask in the conversation.

6. HOSTING INSTEAD OF ENTERTAINING.
Hosting indicates that the guest's needs are being determined and met. Entertaining suggests preparation of your house in decorating, gourmet foods, and impressive perfection. Hospitality focuses on offering a congeniality in the atmosphere of the home.

7. PREPARE YOUR CHILDREN.
Talk to the the kids to ready them for opportunities to be hospitable. Practice table conversation that values listening more than talking. Teach them to serve by cleaning the table and cleaning the kitchen while you commit your attention to your guests. Remind them how often others serve them. Encourage your children to love donning an apron to serve. Over the years, my children have been privileged to serve each week in our local church, at the nearby boys' home, on the mission field in India and later Columbia, South America, at a WWII Veteran's Luncheon, a three day educational event with over 700 adults, a mission of mercy two day dental ministry, a medical supply ministry banquet and numerous opportunities in our home.

Evaporate Stress with New Habits
When the focus is on serving instead of being self-conscience or striving to impress others, the stress of hospitality evaporates. Serving and ministering to others transforms the giver even more than the

recipient. When considering ways to nurture in your home, few habits are more impactful than hospitality habits.

⁓

Memory Making - Doing Life Together

In conclusion to these thoughts of warm-heartedness that make a home hum, remember that those who live in your home are the people that you are doing life with right now.

Indulge in the rhythms of the seasons, of celebrations, of traditions, of birthdays, of graduations and of just regular days.

Aim to sit together for meals.

Take road trips for the fun of it, to make memories and soak in long interrupted hours for talking.

Create a memory box for each family member saving memorabilia honoring them.

Make every birthday a birthday week or month.

Listen to books together.

Tell each other about what you are reading as if you have your own family book club.

Read books out loud together.

Help each other get to where they are going on time.

Make an extra sandwich if you know someone is going to need a lunch.

Practice technology free meals as well as creating conversation spaces.

Try international foods together. (I taught everyone how to make sushi this past Thanksgiving Day. Why? Because I could. Everyone loved it. I might have started a new tradition.)

Celebrate snow days. Take pictures. Go sledding. Ride a huge cardboard box down the best hill in the neighborhood.

Sit by the fire.

Make hot chocolate.

Take Sabbaticals. Rest together.

Worship together.

Read Scripture out loud together.

Sing together.

Play together.

Volunteer together.

Be loyal always.

Give Hugs.

Ask those that live in your home "What makes you feel loved? Cared for? Nurtured? If you are married, ask your husband, "What can I do to help you?" Some time ago when my children were all going to their orthodontist, I remember telling him that most mornings I ask my husband what I can do for him that day. He almost fell on the floor. This seemed so common to me, but not to him. It made me think that we need to be thoughtful of those we live with. It is not that we should be a doormat or embrace entitlement or encourage a lack of responsibility. Be sensitive to serving others that actually live with us in small and meaningful ways.

In conclusion, my prayer is that you would ask God to use your dorm, your apartment, your home, your yard, your patio or your kitchen table for the purpose of showing irresistible, generous hospitality to your family, your friends, your neighbors, your church community and even strangers. Remember it is a lifestyle which requires a mind-set. The point is to steward the material things that God has given me and you to further the kingdom. God will bless you richly.

Determine to be the healthiest version of yourself by asking God to reveal areas needing adjustment. Overview your goals for clean-ing and cooking and hospitality. Establish routines and rhythms that create the harmony God intended in your home. Whether you make slight adjustments or substantial ones, aim for a calmer home envi-ronment where others enter and hear the hum of your home.

Discussion Questions for a Group Study

Journeying together to develop routines that establish the rhythms of healthy allows for the Godly living that ensures the hum in our home. The concepts discussed in *Hum of the Home* offer a wonderful opportunity to network and grow in a small group. Answer these questions as you read through this book.

Chapter 1 - Healthy You
Grab a notebook or empty journal. This book contains three sections. Allow for reflection and note-taking. Growing into a healthy you requires accessing all areas of yourself and thinking about what is healthy and what needs attention.
Why is it important to prepare to do our work well?

What happens when I am not prepared?

How can I gain wisdom from God about my daily life?
Look up Proverbs 3:6.

How important is it to plan?

Look up Proverbs 13:16.

Look up 2 Peter 1:5-8. List the qualities that God wants you to pursue.

Why should I pursue these qualities?

What do I need to do to be healthy in all parts of myself?

List ways that you are healthy and not healthy in each of these categories:

Physical Health

    Healthy

    Not healthy

Spiritual Health

    Healthy

    Not healthy

Relational Health

Healthy

Not healthy

Mental Health

Healthy

Not healthy

Emotional Health

    Healthy

    Not healthy

What else does the Bible say about being a healthy you?

Write out your plans for the next season as you work toward being the healthiest version of yourself.

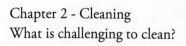

Chapter 2 - Cleaning
What is challenging to clean?

How do you organize your daily cleaning tasks? Explain your plan.

What is working? What is not working?

How do you organize your weekly cleaning?

What is working?

What is not working?

What seasonal cleaning do you and your family do? List.

What areas would you like to see cleaned yearly? Twice a year?

How could I speed clean? What areas could I speed clean?

Is my car clean? What is my method for keeping my car clean? From what I am reading, what habits can I add?

Am I happy with how I process my laundry?

Do I store things at my parents' home?

Do I have a storage unit?

Look up these verses and make notes.

Prov 31:27
Prov 9:9
Prov 31:17

What rhythms work well in cleaning my home?

Am I teaching my children to work?

What needs to be purged from my home?

List tips that you find work for you.

What do I need to do to grow in my routines?

Chapter 3 - Food
How organized are my pantry and my refrigerator?

Are there foods that need to be rotated to the front?

Make a personal list for needs in your pantry.

Make a personal list for needs in your refrigerator.

Do you think it would be helpful to stock up on non-perishables? Create a list of items for your home that you could stock up in your storage areas.

What advantages would I have if I bulk cooked?

List foods that my family enjoys having repeatedly. Could these be made in bulk?

What foods could I make if I was packing a cooler? or lunches?

What foods could I put in a snack drawer?

List what these verses indicate about generosity.

Galatians 6:9

Is it important to keep working on the systems in my home so that I can be at my very best?

Proverbs 22:9

Can I feed more people well if I am more organized in shopping for my food and preparing it?

⟶

Chapter 4 - Hospitality
In what ways do I practice hospitality in my home?

In what ways am I generous?

How do I prepare for having others in my home for a meal?

How do I prepare to have others in for an overnight?

How do I prepare for Christmas? Are there ideas that I can add to my preparations?

Have you ever felt isolated? When? Does hospitality allow people to feel less vunerable?

Have you enjoyed being in someone's home for a meal? Overnight? What made it wonderful?

Have you had a poor experience being in someone's home for a meal or overnight? What could have been done differently?

What can I do to make memories?

What are some of my favorite traditions?

What does 1 Peter 4:9 say about hospitality?

From reading this book and working through the ideas with this group, in what ways have you been challenged to grow?

Recipes for Cooking Ahead and Freezer Meals

⌇⟶

Most freezer meals can keep about 4-6 months. Rotate items in your freezer to ensure that you don't let food go to waste. Pull food forward as you evaluate the inventory in your freezer. The following recipes are just a sampling of foods that work for cooking ahead and freezer meals.

Some people have asked me if taking the time to cook ahead and make freezer meals is worth it. It really depends on whether you want to save money and time as well as improve your nutrition. If your answer to this is yes, then you should prepare freezer meals. This is not intended to be a recipe book, but just a few easy-to-do favorites. There is a plethora of ideas in cookbooks and online.

⌇⟶

Leah's Recipes

⌇⟶

Chocolate Chip Cookie Balls

5 cups all-purpose flour
2 tsps. baking soda
2 tsps. salt
2 cups butter or Crisco
1.5 cups sugar
1.5 cups brown sugar

2 tsp. vanilla extract

4 eggs

2 (12 oz) packages of your favorite chips. I like to mix two kinds like
   white chocolate and mini semi-chocolate.

1-2 cups chopped pecans

2 tsp. ground cinnamon

Preheat oven to 375 degrees. If necessary, prepare your cookie sheet
by buttering it or placing waxed paper down. Some cookie sheets do
not need any preparation.

Combine flour, baking soda and salt. Set aside.

Combine butter, sugar, brown sugar and vanilla extract.

Beat until creamy. Beat in eggs.

Slowly add flour mixture. Stir in nuts and chocolate chips.

Using a medium cookie scoop, drop level teaspoons onto a cookie
sheet.

Cookies can be placed close together without touching. Place in freezer for about an hour. Place a dozen cookie balls in a freezer quart bag.
Stack in freezer. Take out as needed and follow cooking directions below. (I hope that you successfully hide these cookie dough balls from
people that like frozen cookie dough.)

Bake at 375 degrees for about 10 minutes. Each oven heats differently,
so it is best to turn the light on while the cookies are baking. Pull them
out when they are lightly browned.

Makes approximately ten dozen.

Mr. Tim's Famous Lasagna

The short story behind this recipe is that my husband made this lasagna for me on our second date. I was seriously impressed. I thought, wow, he can cook. Later, he told me that this was the only thing that he knew how to cook. About a month later, he asked me to marry him. We were married eight months after our first date. He is confident that this spectacular lasagna helped him seal the deal. Give it a try and see if you are impressed too.

2 lb. lean ground beef or ground turkey
2 jars Prego meat sauce (or your favorite flavor)
1 large container (24oz) of small curd cottage cheese
1 pkg Sargento sliced swiss cheese
1 pkg Sargento shredded mozarella cheese
1 pkg Sargento shredded cheddar cheese
1 pkg Sargento shredded parmesan cheese
1 box lasagna noodles

Cook as directed so you are working with wet noodles. Add oil to water as you prepare noodles.

Cook meat. Drain. Mix meat with sauce in a medium bowl.

Spread a layer of meat/sauce on bottom of a deep 9x13 pan. (The first year of our marriage I bought two very deep pans intended for broiling. While I use them for making bacon, I also use them for deep dish lasagna.)

Add layer of noodles. Add 2/3 container of cottage cheese.
Add 1/3 of other cheeses except the Parmesan cheese.

Repeat twice. meat/sauce, noodles, cottage cheese, other cheeses.

Aim to finish off with meat sauce and Parmesan cheese. Freeze.

When you are ready to cook, take out of freezer and bake for one and a half hours. This is so perfect for cooking a day ahead. Reheat the day you serve it. The first day it can be soupy, so it needs to firm up and be reheated. This dish is just the thing to take when you need to share a meal out, prepare a meal at your house, or be ready for a house full of guests. Add a salad and a dessert. Instantly, you are the hero.

Manicotti

1 box manicotti shells
1/2 lb. ground turkey
1/2 lb. lean ground beef
1/2 lb. fresh sausage
1 pkg shredded Parmesan cheese
1 egg
1 jar favorite spaghetti sauce

Fry the meat. Drain. While meat is frying, cook the noodles. Scramble egg. Add meat while warm along with the Parmesan cheese. Mix thoroughly. Set aside. In low flat pan, spread 1/4 of the spaghetti sauce. Stuff the cooked shells with meat sauce and place beside one another in the pan. When complete, spread the sauce on the center of the manicotti. Cover with aluminum foil.
    Freeze.
    Take out of freezer when ready to cook. Cook for 45 minutes at 350 degrees. This is a great dish to prepare ahead.
    Serve with fresh salad.

Stuffed shells are easy. Vary the meat mix and types of shells.

Meatballs

1 lb. ground turkey
1 cup Italian bread crumbs
1/3 cup minced onions
1 egg, slightly beaten
pepper and salt to taste
1 tsp. Worcestershire sauce

Combine turkey, bread crumbs, onion, egg, parsley, pepper, salt, and Worcestershire sauce. This mixture needs to be fairly firm, so add more bread crumbs if necessary. Shape into 1-inch balls. Cook in oven at 350 degrees for 30 minutes. Remove meatballs. Let cool. Freeze.

Reheat when needed.

Meatloaf

I grew up with meatloaf being a frequent main dish at the end of the week. Often a pound of ground beef would expand when tasty leftovers were added to feed our family of six. My kids love meatloaf, so I am trying to add it into our routine more often.

2 lbs. lean ground beef or ground turkey
1 onion chopped in small pieces
2 garlic cloves, minced
1 tsp. salt
2 eggs
1/2 cup milk
1 cup parmesan cheese
2 slices bread, toasted and finely crumbled

Topping:
1 cup ketchup
6 tbsp. brown sugar
1 tsp. dry mustard
1 dash hot sauce

Combine all ingredients and mix well. Shape into a bread pan. As an alternative, line your bread pan with heavy duty foil. Shape meatloaf into the roll that can be frozen separately outside the pan. If you want to eat immediately, bake in a preheated 375 degree oven for 1 hour or until thoroughly cooked (options include adding 1/2 cup corn, real bacon pieces, sausage bits, diced celery, or chopped peppers).

Mix sauce items. Spread on meatloaf. Freeze uncooked.
    Remove from freezer. Preheat oven to 350 degrees. Cook for 1.5 hours. Serve with mashed potatoes.

Chicken
Cook chicken on the bone or boneless, skinless breasts.
    Process the chicken so it is shredded or cubed.

Bag chicken in quart freezer bags to add to recipes.

Option: Add cooked rice or quinoa or beans or your family's favorite vegetables to bag of cooked chicken. This allows you to have a complete meal ready to go. Brown rice is the best for freezer meals.

Ground Meat

Cooked ground meat. When I am cooking for a few months, it would not be unusual for me to cook up 20-30 pounds of ground turkey or lean beef. Drain and then freeze in quart bags. So many meals call for cooked ground meat. Think of the time this takes on the front of a recipe. Think of the quicker clean up when you don't have to fry the meat and clean up the dishes.

Garden Vegetables

Select vegetables that you and your family would enjoy off-season.

Some vegetables and fruit can be blanched and frozen in freezer bags.

Others can be just frozen directly. It is easy to look up each vegetable online and determine how to freeze. Our family loves tomatoes, okra, beans of all kinds, peas, blueberries, and peaches.

Hawaiian Haystack
From the kitchen of my mom, Aloha Vance

This meal has been served at all of our rehearsal dinners. We eat it whenever we are together with the 26 extended family members. If you can't make the party, you will be very sad. I served this at a deacon party in my home about three years ago. People are asking for a repeat party with the same menu. So, the next Hawaiian Haystack party will happen in June. This menu along with the Mexican Party Bar is great for groups of any size.

Being a guest is so easy because you just bring a single ingredient in one category. When creating a sign up sheet, I think about how much each item will cost and sort it out evenly. For example, I estimate that each person signing up will spend about $10. This means for a party of twenty, four people might need to bring chicken.

Once you determine how many guests will attend, the portion sizes can be adjusted. Remember when calculating the meat, allow for a third of a pound per person. If you are feeding all males, add some extra. If you are feeding teenage boys, you should just double the recipe.

Hawaiian Haystack (feeds 20)
Rice (I use my 20 cup rice cooker which makes enough for 15-20 people. Estimate about a cup of rice per person. Rice should be fresh and hot when served. If you don't own a rice cooker, prepare on the stove top.)

Cooked Chicken - 10 pounds (Cook chicken ahead. Shred or cut into diced pieces. If you are in a hurry, you can pick up shredded chicken at your favorite barbecue location.)

green pepper - 6 - red or yellow, chopped or diced
green onion - one bunch, chopped small
celery - 2 stems chopped small
tomatoes - 6 chopped
pineapple- 5 cans - (tidbits work best)

coconut - 2 pounds - shredded
macadamia nuts - 24oz - chopped
chow mien noodles - 5 cans
cheddar cheese - 5 pounds of grated cheddar or mixed
poultry (chicken or turkey) gravy

I buy the powdered version from Sam's. You need to be prepared to make at least two containers of this gravy. Your guests will love the gravy and need more.

To serve this menu:
Start the line with large plates, warm rice, chicken, all other ingredients except cheese and gravy. I usually line up the ingredients like the above list which places the salty items first with the sweet at the end. After selecting all items, top with grated cheese and gravy. Caution eager guests to start off with small portions as your haystack size may overwhelm you. This is such a fun food anytime. Add to the happiness by decorating and dressing with a Hawaiian theme.

Mexican Party Bar (serves 20ish)
This is also an easy and popular party menu. Once again, each guest brings one ingredient in a large quantity. It allows for preparation ahead of time which encourages better hospitality. Feel free to vary the ingredients and portions to your needs.

tortilla bowls (20)
flour tortillas - small (30) and large (20)
brown rice with cilantro and lime (25 cups)
shredded beef (10 pounds)

carnitas shredded pork (10 pounds)
shredded chicken (10 pounds)
pinto beans in chili sauce (5 cans)
black beans (3 cans)
shredded cheese (5 pounds of grated cheddar cheese)
shredded lettuce greens (2 heads of romaine)
salsa (5-6 jars or more) - Be sure to mark these "Mild" and "Hot."
grilled corn (or white corn - 6 cans)
guacamole (enough)
tortilla chips (3 large bags)
sour cream (2 16 oz. containers)

Fun it up with decorations and bright festive clothing! Enjoy!

Salads in a Jar (serves 8)
Seriously, one of the best ideas for cooler eating or just easy eating at home is the salad in a jar. The variety is endless. For several years I have tried numerous recipes until I settled on this order of foods. Remember it is a stacking game.

Preparation Instructions:
Prep ingredients which means cutting, peeling, washing the veggies/fruits.
Boil the pasta, quinoa or rice.
Lay out all the ingredients in the order of the layers.
Layer your choice of ingredients into the jars and store them in the refrigerator. In no time, you have easy to enjoy salads prepared ahead.

Layer 1:
Wide mouth 1 quart Mason jars - 8 jars
Poppy seed dressing or your favorite - 2 bottles
Pour about 1/4 cup of dressing into the bottom.

Layer 2:
Layer crisp vegetables next. Choose your favorite vegetables cleaned and chopped and ready to eat. Favorites at my house are seedless cucumbers, tomatoes, red onion, asparagus, celery, peppers and carrots. Imagine vegetables that can be pickled or are not damaged by being soggy.

Layer 3:
Select mushrooms, zucchini, squash, beans, peas, corn, broccoli for the next layer.

Layer 4:
More fragile ingredients such as hard boiled eggs and cheese (feta, gouda, cheddar create the next layer. My personal favorite is always small curd cottage cheese. Sometimes I carry the boiled eggs and grated cheese in an outside bag to add to the overall freshness of my salad.

Layer 5 (optional):
If you would like to add a more substantial layer, add couscous, quinoa, or my favorite canned chicken.

Layer 6:
The last layer is at the top of the jar to ensure that it is mostly dry. Select your green layer from romaine, spinach, or arugula or a combination of greens. Nuts such as almonds and pine nuts are our favorites.

One of my talented kitchen friends, Janine Wilkins, shared some of her most well-loved recipes. We met when our boys began to work together as a winning Parliamentary debate team in STOA (Christian

Homeschool Speech and Debate). Janine and I organize and run kitchens that feed hundreds of adults and students for 3-4 day tournaments. Most recently, I have worked in Janine's kitchens. I am not ashamed to say that we feed people well and I know that they feel loved.

Let me share one very heartwarming story about loving people with food. Usually on the last day of the tournament, students find out the results of 2-3 days of competition. Some advance to out rounds. Others don't. Saturdays are emotionally charged days. Knowing that more students are disappointed than those who are happily moving forward, Janine prepared a popcorn bar. As announcements finished and sadnesses was settling, she called out that the popcorn bar was open. With a cup of popcorn, the kids could go down the table picking up their favorite toppings. This thoughtful timing of a fun snack brought lots of smiles.

Enjoy a few of her favorite ideas.

Make Ahead Recipes from Janine Wilkins' Kitchen

Combine the dishes below into one pan as a meal for two:
Chicken Cordon Bleu
Rice Pilaf
Green Beans
Candied Carrots
This is a very easy meal that is a big crowd pleaser and works per-fectly to fill the freezer. You can fit the entire meal for two people

in one aluminum half steam table pan. It makes a very appreciated gift this way, whether hot or frozen!

Chicken Cordon Bleu:
Boneless Chicken Breasts (best if never have been frozen)
sliced ham (rectangle package is easiest)
Swiss cheese
butter
Italian style bread crumbs
olive oil

Pound out each breast a bit so it's easier to roll. For as many pieces as you want to do, cut a chunk of the swiss (about an ounce) or fold up a slice. Wrap the cheese in ham like a little package. Cover the bottom of an aluminum half steam table pan with olive oil. Dip both sides of the breast in olive oil. Wrap the chicken around the package and roll in bread crumbs. Place with seam side down in the pan. Place a pat of butter on each piece.

Cover and bake for 30 minutes at 350 degrees. Remove cover and cook for another 30 minutes. Check to make sure they are browned and cooked all the way through.

You can freeze them after they are cooked. If you use "never been frozen" chicken, then you can freeze them raw. If raw, they take about 2 hours to cook from frozen (cover for half the cooking time). If they've been cooked already, then they take about 40 minutes-1 hour to heat through. Keep covered the whole time.

To do this for a large crowd or to make ahead, do as an assembly line. Children love to make the "packages." I've used these for many large events. It's wonderful to have the main dish ready to go.

⟨⁓⟩

Rice Pilaf
There are many ways to make this easy and delicious side dish. This is just the way I make it.

Make brown rice (I use my rice cooker). I like to add wild rice or jasmine for some color. You can also break up some spaghetti and brown it in butter, then add a little water and sauté until cooked and add it again, just for color.

Sauté a sliced onion in a stick of butter (for about 2 cups of rice). When onion is translucent, add the rice. Make some broth with a half a cup of water and "Better than Boullion" or other tasty chicken base.

Add salt and pepper to taste. Season with onion powder or even minced onion for more flavor. I usually end up adding more butter after I taste it. I haven't tried this recipe with white rice. I like how the brown rice holds up in the freezer.

⟨⁓⟩

Green Beans
For make ahead meals. Get some whole frozen green beans. sauté a sliced onion in butter. Add the beans. Season with salt and pepper and onion powder. Let the beans stay frozen.

⟨⁓⟩

Candied Carrots

Boil whole baby carrots until tender. Don't overcook them. Drain. In the empty pot, put a stick of butter (for about a bag of carrots) and a half cup of brown sugar. Melt the sugar and stir. Add the carrots.

To freeze with cooked chicken: Just portion out each item into foil pans. They can just be popped into the oven until heated or dumped onto a plate and be microwaved! Heat and eat!

For raw chicken: Don't mix with the other food. Pan up all the sides together. So when it's time to eat you can just cook the chicken as directed and put the sides pan in the oven for the last 45 minutes. Easy Peasy!!

Sausage and Peppers

An Italian classic. When frozen in portions, it can be served over pasta, a baked potato, or on crusty bread as a sub sandwich.

Boil Italian sausages until cooked. Let them cool. Slice into half inch slices.

For a pound of sausage use 2 bell peppers (any color) and 2 onions and 2 cloves of garlic. Slice peppers and onions and chop garlic. Sauté in olive oil or toss with olive oil and bake in the oven until soft and roasted looking.

When the peppers and onions are soft add the sliced sausages and sauté for a few minutes until fully combined.

Freeze in individual or family sized portions.

Spinach Meatballs
ground beef
minced garlic
Italian bread crumbs
chopped frozen spinach
grated Italian cheese
(optional: mozzarella cheese)
eggs
basil, oregano, salt, and pepper

These measurements are approximate and are to taste for about a pound of meat. But you'll need to make MUCH MORE because they are so yummy and easy to eat! A complete meal in a ball!

Mix together beef, 2 cloves of garlic minced, 24 eggs, and a handful of grated cheese. Add seasonings. If you're unsure of how much, start with a half teaspoon of each and then fry a little tiny hamburger on the stove and see how you like it.

Drain the spinach very well and squeeze it out. Add to meat. When that's all mixed add breadcrumbs starting with a cup. Keep mixing and adding bread crumbs until it's a good consistency. Not too firm, still a little sticky, but not too sticky either. Your hands shouldn't be all gooey.

Make meatballs whatever size you desire onto parchment. Bake until almost done on cookie sheets. Drain the grease and then freeze on cookie sheets if possible. Then freeze in Ziploc bags.

These are amazing to have on hand. They are perfect as a little snack or as the main dish. An easy meal would be to pair with buttered pasta.

You could also sauté garlic in olive oil and put on spaghetti, then add grated cheese. That would go very nicely with meatballs. Of course any tomato sauce on pasta is a natural with meatballs.

Notes

Introduction:
p. xviii, Staci Eldridge, *Becoming Myself* (Colorado Springs, CO: David Cook, 2014), pg. 69

Chapter 1 Healthy You
p. 1, Tyndall, *New Living Translation* NLT (Carol Stream, IL: Tyndall, 1996)
p. 3, Crossway, *English Standard Version* ESV (Wheaton, IL: Crossway, 2006)
p. 3, Tyndall, *New Living Translation* NLT
p. 4, Tyndall, *New Living Translation* NLT
p. 16, Ruth Haley Barton, *Sacred Rhythms* (Downers Grove, IL: InterVarsity Press, 2006) pg. 187.
p. 20, Crossway, *English Standard Version* ESV

Chapter 2 Cleaning
p. 23, Tyndall, *New Living Translation* NLT
p. 28, Crossway, *English Standard Version* ESV
p. 31, Tyndall, *New Living Translation* NLT

p. 40, Marie Kondo, *The Life Changing Magic of Tidying Up: The Japanese Art of Decluttering and Organizing* (Berkeley, CA: Ten Speed Press, 2014)

Chapter 3 Food
p. 71, Crossway, *English Standard Version* ESV
p. 87, Crossway, *English Standard Version* ESV
p. 94, Tyndall, *New Living Translation* NLT
p. 97, Tyndall, *New Living Translation* NLT

Chapter 4 Hospitality
p. 109, Crossway, *English Standard Version* ESV
p. 111, Crossway, *English Standard Version* ESV
p. 112, Crossway, *English Standard Version* ESV
p. 123, Crossway, *English Standard Version* ESV

Notes

Notes